How to Write Better Letters

Cherry Chappell is an independent public relations practitioner and writer. Trained originally as a journalist, she regularly reverts to type, writing features for national newspapers and magazines. Cherry's first book, *Minding Your Own Business: Survival Strategies for Starting Up on Your Own*, was published in September 2004. She has friends all over the world and so is an inveterate letter-writer.

The Penguin Writers' Guides

PENGUIN WRITERS' GUIDES

How to Write Better Letters

CHERRY CHAPPELL

PENGUIN BOOKS

PENGUIN BOOKS

Published by the Penguin Group
Penguin Books Ltd, 80 Strand, London WC2R ORL, England
Penguin Group (USA) Inc., 375 Hudson Street, New York, New York 10014, USA
Penguin Group (Canada), 90 Eglinton Avenue East, Suite 700, Toronto, Ontario, Canada M4P 2Y3
(a division of Pearson Penguin Canada Inc.)
Penguin Ireland, 25 St Stephen's Green, Dublin 2, Ireland
(a division of Penguin Books Ltd)
Penguin Group (Australia), 250 Camberwell Road, Camberwell, Victoria 3124, Australia
(a division of Pearson Australia Group Pty Ltd)
Penguin Books India Pvt Ltd, 11 Community Centre, Panchsheel Park, New Delhi – 110 017, India
Penguin Group (NZ), cnr Airborne and Rosedale Roads, Albany, Auckland 1310, New Zealand
(a division of Pearson New Zealand Ltd)
Penguin Books (South Africa) (Pty) Ltd, 24 Sturdee Avenue, Rosebank,
Johannesburg 2196, South Africa

Penguin Books Ltd, Registered Offices: 80 Strand, London WC2R ORL, England

www.penguin.com

First published 2006
2

Extract from *A Profound Secret* by Josceline Dimbleby, published by Doubleday/Black Swan,
reprinted by permission of the Random House Group Ltd. Extract from *Dear Mariella* by
Mariella Frostrup, published by Bloomsbury, reprinted by permission of the author.
Extract from *Martha Gellhorn: A Life* by Caroline Moorehead, published by
Chatto & Windus, reprinted by permission of the Random House Group Ltd.
Every effort has been made to trace copyright holders but this has not been possible
in all cases. If notified, the publishers will be pleased to rectify any omissions at the
earliest opportunity.

The moral right of the author has been asserted

Set in 11/13 pt Adobe Minion
Typeset by Rowland Phototypesetting Ltd, Bury St Edmunds, Suffolk
Printed in England by Clays Ltd, St Ives plc

ISBN-13: 978–0–141–02276–5
ISBN-10: 0–141–02276–0

For Mansel and Joan

Contents

Letter from the Author

Dear Reader,

Not long ago, I sat opposite a young foreign student on an underground train and idly watched him as he opened a letter. His face lit up. Photos fell out. He whooped. He then read his letter, smiling and even laughing out loud at one point. His delight cheered me up, along with everyone else around us. When he left the train, still hugging his letter, I felt he would find time later to read it again – and maybe a third time. Perhaps he was homesick and the letter was from his family; maybe it was from a special girl. We'll never know, but the incident reminded me of the importance of personal letters. A handwritten letter or note, perhaps to a friend who is going through a tough time, is much more intimate and caring than an email or a text message, and can be read again and again. A good luck note may give the recipient confidence.

There are many other reasons why letters remain an important means of communication. Despite mobiles, land lines, broadband and text messaging, there are still occasions when it is much more appropriate to write a letter. In an official sphere – for instance, when you are making a complaint – a letter has a legal presence. In other instances, a letter shows a commitment and a strength of purpose that an email message may not. Then, sometimes, we need to send a covering letter for forms we must fill in, for that important job application perhaps.

Unlike speaking to someone directly or on the phone, the value of writing a letter is that it is *not* immediate; it gives the writer time to structure the communication, select the right words, consider the tone and style, polish it, maybe put it to one side and read it again, reflect and ponder, so that the final version is precisely what you wish it to be.

Sometimes letters are better written on paper and posted with a stamp, while others can as easily be despatched as an email. Whatever the means of delivery, writers will wish to express themselves fluently and appropriately. You will probably want to give special meaning to a personal letter, and ensure that it is one the recipient will relish reading and perhaps treasure. On the other hand, you will need to ensure that business and official letters contain all the necessary information, but are presented with clarity and brevity. Busy people need to understand in the shortest possible time what your letter is about and what you require of them. You are more likely to receive a prompt and positive response if your letter is easy to read and concise.

Some people adore writing letters – I certainly do. Others, for a variety of reasons, find writing letters a chore to postpone as long as possible, or something to be drafted, redrafted and worried over. Still other people enjoy scribbling a note to a chum, but seize up when faced with an official invitation. Most of us find writing a letter of condolence, so important to someone who has recently been bereaved, the hardest one of all.

This guide is designed to help you enjoy – yes, *enjoy* – the process of letter-writing. If you are writing about a job, it's probably wise to ask someone to check for spelling mistakes and other howlers but, for most other kinds of letter, it is better to go ahead and write – errors and all – than never to have written at all.

With best wishes,
Yours sincerely,

Cherry Chappell

Chelsea, London 2006

Acknowledgements

I am immensely grateful for all the help, time and support so many people have given to me in writing this book. In particular, I would like to thank:

Andie Airfix of Satori; Kevin Allen; Theresa Britt of the Open University; The Duke of Buccleuch; The Cornish Hospices; Victoria Crawford; David and Sheila Crawley; Gareth Davies and Dan Mars from the Cleft Lip & Palate Association; Malcolm J. Dyson of M & M Carpet Contractors Ltd; Nick Elliott, director of international business, Romeike International; Richard Elsen of Bell Yard Communications; Shernaz Engineer of Verity; Nick Gundry; C. Hamblet; Daniel Hannan, MEP for South East England; Christobel Hargraves and Steven Dowling of the National Confidential Enquiry into Patient Outcome and Death; Mrs Valerie Harrison; Christine Herbertson; Majid Ichalhane; John Jackson-Okolo; Jackie Jennings; Marzbeen and Paurrush Jila; Councillor Jenny Kingsley; Jill Lee of Artbeat; Patricia Marriott; Dr Vivien Martin; Dr Susan Mayor; Ann Mealor of the Chartered Institute of Public Relations; Laura Morris; Christine Moulié; Ali Musa of MacMedicine; Tony Northcott of the Trading Standards Institute; Steve Pound, MP for Ealing North, and his parliamentary manager, Sophie Hosking; Stephen Pritchard of the *Observer*; Paul Scott-Lee, QPM DL, Chief Constable of West

Midlands Police; Andy Simpson, readers' letters editor of the *Daily Mail*; Julia Smith; Peter Lippiatt and Catherine Condor of Smythson of Bond Street; Carole Stone; Corinne Sweet; Gillian Swift; Claire Thomas, HR Manager of Penguin Books; Tristan Vanhegan.

1

Signing Up to the Basics

1.1 WHAT LETTERS ARE FOR

Let's consider briefly what letters are for, be they written and posted or sent by email. By and large, they are communications of facts, feelings, ideas and requests, and sometimes of complaint, care, concern or gratitude. This was the purpose of writing this book: to help you become a more fluent writer, making you not only aware of what you wish to express but also able to anticipate the likely response from the recipient.

Letters can rarely be written to a formula, and it stands out a mile if they are constructed in this way. The best letters are those where the voice and personality of the writer can be plainly heard. There are examples throughout this book, many of them authentic and published by kind permission of the correspondents. They are there to give you an idea of how such letters might be written, rather than tight little patterns to copy out word by word.

Each subject area has its own chapter, with authoritative input from expert advisers as well as pertinent examples. To help you find your way through the book, the chapters fall into three main subject areas, although obviously there are some cross-overs. The sections are:

- *Your working life:* setting out a contract or agreement letter, applying for a job, writing a reference, and the clever and polite way of writing and sending emails (Chapters 2 to 5).
- *Your private/social life:* designing invitations for family events, replying to the invitations you receive, sending thank-you letters, writing when someone is ill or has died, and writing love letters (Chapters 6 to 9).
- *Your public life:* raising money or support for charities, writing to politicians or newspaper editors, or making complaints about goods and services (Chapters 10 to 13).

Throughout, attention is paid to what our society deems to be correctness. Some of the 'rules' of even twenty or thirty years ago are now so outmoded as to be comical and are gradually dropping away. Others just come across as old-fashioned courtesy, which is something that may be greatly appreciated by the recipient of the letter. Still more are highly practical, and aid easier reading. For example, when your letter has to stand out in the pile – at a newspaper office or in a politician's in-tray – a good clear presentation can be very important to its impact.

There are a few occasions when it is worth ensuring

that your communication is correct in the old manner – a job application letter for example, or an invitation to a wedding or a prestigious event. Where it is important that you don't make spelling or grammatical mistakes, or other howlers, it is a good idea to ask someone you trust to proofread your letter for you. Other than these more specialist letters, the essential thing is to write . . . and not just think about doing so. The following sections are not 'rules' in the accepted sense. They are guidelines to be used if you wish.

1.2 WRITING PAPER

There is so much choice. You can choose any colour, with pre-printed borders, or plain. For the more formal letter you will probably wish to select a paper that is fairly neutral in colour: pale blue, grey, cream or white. In weight, the best papers, which should take fountain pen ink as well as ballpoint pen or computer printer ink, are normally between 115 and 160 grams. Some of the grander stationers still produce papers in the old imperial sizes: Quarto, Imperial, Kings and Duke. Otherwise the most common sizes are A4 (particularly for business use), A5 and A6 for personal correspondence.

If you are having your notepaper personalized in the UK, you will probably have your address at the top, but not your name (in the USA, people have their names at the top, but not their address. Businesses show both, on either side of the Atlantic). On personal stationery, addresses are usually centred, with the phone number shown below, or the address on the right-hand corner and the phone number on the left. It is rare for commas to be shown. This makes for a cleaner, crisper, more modern appearance:

> 12 Philadelphia Road
> London SW.. ...
> 020 7350 1234

or

Telephone: 020 7350 1234   12 Philadelphia Road
                                            London SW.. ...

Black and dark blue remain the favourite colours for inks but you can let your imagination stretch – scarlet on oyster? blue on pink? – and your pocket with it. You can aspire to finely milled papers with watermarks, engraved letter headings with die stamps specially made for your address (you can tell the real thing by the raised surface of the type on the finished page), tissue-lined envelopes, or hand engraved motifs both on paper and on the back of the envelopes. Smythson of Bond Street, which has been producing stationery since 1887, has received some particularly extravagant orders over the decades, including one from Indian maharajas, who called for their coronets and monograms to be inlaid with mother of pearl.

1.3 CORRESPONDENCE CARDS

These postcard-sized single flat cards have mush-
roomed in popularity. They are usually personalized,
with the sender's name, address and phone number –
and probably email address too – running across the
top, followed by a single line, allowing plenty of room
for short messages or informal invitations. For
example:

Charles Hearthrug, 12 Philadelphia Road, London SW.. ...
Telephone: 020 7350 1234 Email: charlie@hearthrug.com

1.4 ENVELOPES

The most attractive presentation is to have an envelope
that matches the paper. As a guideline, large A4 envelopes and third A4 with self-sealed flaps are most suited
to business use. Personal correspondence looks
smarter in smaller envelopes, with flaps which are
pointed, and usually require licking to seal them. At
the time of writing the Post Office does not have any
restrictions on sizes, but the very large and the very
tiny do stand a chance of being torn or lost in the
bottom of mailbags.

Take care in addressing the envelopes. Write – or
better, print – the address as clearly as possible, and
always ensure that you use the correct postcode. If
you are writing to someone on a personal basis but
at their business address, always mark the envelope
'Private & Confidential' – perhaps on the top left-hand

side above the address – so it won't be opened by a secretary by mistake.

There is no correct format for styling the address. Some people who are handwriting the address like to 'stagger' the lines. For example:

Mr Charles Hearthrug
    12 Philadelphia Road
        London SW.. ...

It's just as correct to align the address, particularly for business use. For example:

Mr Charles Hearthrug
12 Philadelphia Road
London SW.. ...

If you wish, you can add your return address on the back flap of the envelope. This is common practice in many countries but is only occasionally used in the UK. Your address normally appears in one line, rather than 'tiered' as you would write the address of the recipient.

1.5 LAYOUT

There's little point in sending a letter that is hard work to read. A smart crisp presentation for a formal or business letter looks professional and sets the tone. For personal correspondence, you would normally write your address – if it's not printed – on the top right-hand side of the page. If you are writing to a company or a politician, you would then write their name and address underneath but on the left-hand side. There is no need to do this for friends and relations and more informal correspondence.

Business letters tend to be written on one side of the paper only, whereas handwritten letters are frequently written on both sides.

For a business or more formal letter, leave wide margins. This again aids easy reading. Consider allowing at least 2.5 cm (or 1 inch) all around. Some people like to indent their paragraphs. This certainly works for a handwritten letter, but many formal business letters these days are written with paragraphs in 'blocks' with no initial indentation.

By and large, people prefer 'open' punctuation; it makes the page look cleaner. This means that you don't put commas in addresses or full stops between the letters of abbreviations, for instance, RSVP.

Always show the date. The more formal style is to write the day as a number, the month in letters, and the year again in numbers. For example:

12th July 2007

or

12 July 2007

Some business letters use only numerals, e.g. 12/7/07. This may be acceptable in business circles within the UK, but it is worth remembering that other countries have a different order when writing a date, most particularly the USA.

In a business letter you should also display a subject heading or any necessary reference numbers. For example:

12 Europa Road
London SW.. ...

Mr Steve Pound MP
House of Commons
London SW1. ...

24th June 2005

Dear Mr Pound,

'How to Write Better Letters' for Penguin Books

Thank you very much for agreeing to meet me to talk about how to improve letters sent to politicians. I look forward to meeting you at Portcullis House at 11 a.m. on Tuesday, 26th July.

Yours sincerely,

Cherry Chappell

1.6 GREETINGS AND SIGNING OFF

The most common form of greeting is Dear . . . If you don't know the name of the person you are writing to – perhaps you are writing to a company and only know the job title – you would follow 'Dear' with 'Sir' or 'Madam'. If you don't know the gender, you can write 'Dear Sir or Madam'. When you know the name of the person you are writing to, add it in. If it's a close friend, you might start 'My dear . . .' followed by a first name or, if you are closer still, why not start with 'Darling'?

There are some variations if you are writing to very senior members of prominent churches or the upper echelons of the diplomatic service or Royal Family. (See *Titles and Forms of Address* on pages 12 to 18.)

The most usual formats for the pairing of greetings and sign-offs are:

Dear Sir, . . . Yours faithfully,

Dear Mrs Smith, . . . Yours sincerely, (*or* Yours truly,)

Dear Yvonne, . . . Yours sincerely,

or

> Best wishes,
> Yours sincerely,

Notice that commas appear after the greeting and again after the sign-off but before you sign your name.

There was a time when you would sign off a letter to a hereditary peer with the words

I have the honour to remain,
Your lordship's obedient servant,

Unsurprisingly this is now rarely used. There are other sign-offs that are also dropping out of common use, notably:

> Yours truly,
> Your obedient servant,

and

Yours respectfully,

When you sign, you will probably use your first name and surname. However, you would not add your title: Mr, Mrs or Miss or a formal title such as Group Captain or Reverend. If you wish these titles to appear, they should be written neatly underneath. This helps people when they come to reply to your letter. For example:

Yours sincerely,

Henry Ashworth (hand signature)
The Rt Hon Henry Ashworth, MP

or

Yours sincerely,

Emily West
Dr Emily West GP

Signatures can appear on the left or in the centre.

1.7 TITLES AND FORMS OF ADDRESS

When writing to someone who is prominent, it is usual to include any *decorations* they may have – e.g. OBE, KCMG, DBE – or *qualifications* – e.g. GP, FRCS, MA – or *indications of their official appointments* – e.g. JP, MP, QC – alongside their name, with the address which appears at the head of your letter, and again on the envelope. These are honours that people have usually worked hard to achieve, and most will appreciate your use of them. There is no need to use full stops between the letters in the abbreviated form.

There are also many different hereditary titles and appointed titles, all with traditional – and individual – forms of address, the more formal of which you would use on the envelope, and a user-friendly version for your salutation or greeting. The list overleaf outlines only the most frequently used. There are many variations and when in doubt it is courteous to check what is correct and acceptable to your recipient. Secretaries, PAs and libraries are usually very helpful.

When it comes to writing to gentlemen who do not have a title (but may have qualifications) it has become common practice to use 'Mr' rather than 'Esq.' which looks outdated.

Addressing single women remains a challenge. Some women prefer the form Miss, while others loathe it and wish to be addressed as Ms. When in doubt, it is probably the safest to use Miss. Miss accompanied by a maiden name is used in a business setting by many professional women, even after marriage. This may be because their career reputations have been made in their single years, or simply because they are happy to be defined in their own, rather than their husband's name. An example of this is Cherie Booth QC, whose career has continued in that name throughout the time of her husband's Prime Ministership.

There is a not dissimilar challenge in addressing someone who chairs a committee. Men are still often referred to as Chairman, but this cannot be taken for granted. Some are called the Chair or even Chairperson. Very few women are referred to as Chairwoman these days and are usually Chair or Chairperson. When in any doubt, try to check with the secretary of the organization.

Widows retain their late husband's surname but their status is defined by the use of their first name. For example, Mrs James Wright became Mrs Edna Wright on the death of her husband. This is also the correct form for divorcees.

Titles and Forms of Address

Standard Forms

Title	Greeting in a letter	Envelope
Men	Dear Mr Black	Mr Henry Black (or Mr H A Black)
Men *(when name unknown)*	Dear Sir	
Married Women	Dear Mrs Black	Mrs Henry Black (or Mrs H A Black)
Widows or Divorced Women	Dear Mrs Black	Mrs Sophie Black
Single Women	Dear Miss Black	Miss Henrietta Black
Women *(when name unknown)*	Dear Madam	

Professions

Title	Greeting in a letter	Envelope
Doctor (General Practitioner, Junior Hospital Doctors, Consultant Physicians, Anaesthetists, Pathologists)	Dear Dr Practice	Dr Practice MD (and other abbreviations if known)
Consultant Surgeon	Dear Mr Vickers	Mr Roland Vickers FRCS
Chief Constable	Dear Chief Constable/ Dear Sir Thomas	Mr Thomas Edington, Chief Constable/Sir Thomas Edington, Chief Constable
Police Commission (Metropolitan Forces)	Dear Commissioner/ Dear Sir Humphrey	Mr Humphrey Pearl, Commissioner of Police/Sir Humphrey Pearl, Commissioner of Police

Elected Officials

Title	Greeting in a letter	Envelope
The Prime Minister	Dear Prime Minister	The Rt Hon Alison Hope MP, The Prime Minister
The Deputy Prime Minister	Dear Deputy Prime Minister	The Rt Hon James Wright, Deputy Prime Minister

Elected Officials – contd

Title	Greeting in a letter	Envelope
The Chancellor of the Exchequer	Dear Chancellor	The Rt Hon Susan Widge, Chancellor of the Exchequer
Minister	Dear Minister	The Rt Hon Graham Shield MP, Minister of State for Health
City, Borough or District Councillor	Dear Councillor Brave	Councillor Brave

Public Servants

Title	Greeting in a letter	Envelope
Ambassador	Dear Ambassador/Your Excellency	His Excellency, Monsieur Magrit The Ambassador of France
Lord Mayor	Dear Lord Mayor	The Right Honourable/ The Right Worshipful* Lord Mayor of Place
Mayor	Dear Mr Mayor	The Right Worshipful Mayor/The Worshipful Mayor* of Place

* These vary in different cities and towns and so must be checked.
Debrett's Correct Form is useful.

Religious Leaders

Title	Greeting in a letter	Envelope
(Church of England)		
Archbishop	Dear Archbishop/Dear Archbishop John	The Most Reverend and Right Honourable the Archbishop of Place
Bishop	Dear Bishop	The Right Reverend the Bishop of Place
Vicar (or Rector)	Dear Mr/Mrs/Miss Hearty/ Dear Vicar/Dear Rector	The Reverend Chris Hearty
(Roman Catholic)		
The Pope	Your Holiness	His Holiness The Pope
Cardinal	Your Eminence/Dear Cardinal Bloom	His Eminence the Cardinal Archbishop of Place
Monsignor	Dear Monsignor Grey	Monsignor Grey
Priest	Dear Father Leonard	The Reverend Father Leonard
(Jewish)		
The Chief Rabbi	Dear Chief Rabbi	The Very Reverend The Chief Rabbi, Dr Morris Lewen
Rabbi	Dear Rabbi Greenway	Rabbi Lionel Greenway

Religious Leaders – contd

Title	Greeting in a letter	Envelope
(Muslim)		
Imam (Sunni)	Dear Shaykh Saleem	Shaykh Abdel Malik el Fatouaki
Imam (Shia)	Dear Imam Abde Samade ibne Daouode	The Imam of the Mosque of Place
(Hindu)		
Swami	Dear Swami Vivekananda	Swami Vivekananda

Royal Family and Peers

Title	Greeting in a Letter	Envelope
Her Majesty The Queen *write to* The Private Secretary to Her Majesty The Queen	Dear Sir	Private Secretary to Her Majesty The Queen
His Royal Highness The Duke of Edinburgh *write to* The Private Secretary	Dear Sir	Private Secretary to His Royal Highness The Duke of Edinburgh

Title	Greeting in a Letter	Envelope
His Royal Highness The Prince of Wales *write to* The Private Secretary	Dear Sir	Private Secretary to His Royal Highness The Prince of Wales
Duke of Wherever	Dear Duke of [place name]	Duke of [place name]
Duchess	Dear Duchess of [place name]	Duchess of [place name]
Earl	Dear Lord [place name]	The Earl of [place name]
Countess	Dear Lady [place name]	The Countess of [place name]
Baronet	Dear Sir Henry	Sir Henry [surname]
Wife of Baronet	Dear Lady [surname]	Lady [surname]
Life Peer	Dear Lord [surname]	The Lord [surname] of [place name]
Wife of Life Peer	Dear Lady [surname]	The Lady [surname] of [place name]
Knight	Dear Sir Charles	Sir Charles [surname]
Wife of Knight	Dear Lady [surname]	Lady [surname]

Royal Family and Peers – contd

Title	Greeting in a letter	Envelope
Life Peeress	Dear Lady [surname]	The Baroness [surname] of [place name]
Dame	Dear Dame Sophie	Dame Sophie [surname]

* N.B. There are special titles for the children of the above titles, and also variations of these titles in both Scotland and Ireland. The reader is directed to *Debrett's Correct Form* for a full listing.

There are too many abbreviations of civil and military decorations to include a full list here. There are whole books devoted to this subject. However, some of the most common are:

Titles

Bt	Baronet
Esq	Esquire
HM	His (or Her) Majesty
HRH	His (or Her) Royal Highness
Rt Hon	Right Honourable
Rt Revd	Right Reverend

Civil Decorations

CBE	Commander of the British Empire
DBE	Dame of the British Empire
DCM	Distinguished Conduct Medal
KBE	Knight Commander of the British Empire
MBE	Member of the British Empire
OBE	Order of the British Empire

Academia

BA	Bachelor of Arts
BSc	Bachelor of Science
Cantab	of Cambridge University
DD	Doctor of Divinity
MA	Master of Arts
MSc	Master of Science
Oxon	of Oxford University
PhD	Doctor of Philosophy
Prof	Professor

Law

JP	Justice of the Peace
PC	Police Constable

Medical

Dr	Doctor
FRCA	Fellow of the Royal College of Anaesthetists
FRCP	Fellow of the Royal College of Physicians
FRCS	Fellow of the Royal College of Surgeons
GP	General Practitioner
MD	Doctor of Medicine

Politics

MEP	Member of the European Parliament
MP	Member of Parliament
PC	Privy Counsellor
PM	Prime Minister

There are many booby traps for the unwary, not least when people hold a number of different positions and therefore have more than one title or a string of decorations. Knowing which takes precedence is an art form. In my research I came across the following, reproduced in Reader's Digest's *How to Write and Speak Better*.

The following enquiry was addressed to the 'Genuflex' column of the *Daily Telegraph* by Mr Mostyn Sheep-Harris:

> My elder brother Eric, who is in holy orders and also holds medical and dental degrees, joined the police force some 10 years ago and has just been promoted Detective Sergeant. Soon afterwards, through the death of a cousin, he succeeded to the baronetcy.
>
> When writing, how should I address him, as he is a stickler in such matters?

'Genuflex' replied:

> The Revd Det-Sgt Dr Sir Eric Sheep-Harris, Bt, DD, MD, LDS is the correct form. Should your brother be appointed a Privy Councillor, join the Navy, Army or Air Force, or make a pilgrimage to Mecca, please write to me again.

1.8 WRITING STYLE

Beware of pretentiousness. Somehow it simply doesn't ring true. Even if you are writing a love letter – maybe *particularly* if you are writing a love letter – there is no excuse for adopting a fake 'literary' style. Even if the matter about which you are writing is very serious – condolences on the death of a friend or a complaint about skulduggery in high places – there really is no excuse for dropping into purple prose. The art is to express yourself as you would if you were speaking to whoever it is you are writing to: clearly, concisely and with the passion you feel about the situation.

All professions have their own 'speke', that is, their own terminology, common 'shortcuts' and abbreviations. That's fine if you are writing to someone in your profession but it doesn't usually translate to the outer world. It can even become hilarious. My father was a police officer and tended to write even personal letters in an 'I was proceeding along the footpath' kind of way throughout his life. He was much teased about this.

When in doubt, keep it as simple as possible. We have access to a vast and wonderful vocabulary; English is an immensely rich language. Even so, beware of adopting words you would not generally use. If you don't normally bandy the words 'eclectic' or 'panegyric' or whatever, question whether it is really relevant to do so in your letter. Try not to impress (you won't) or show off (it looks corny). Avoid clichés, slang and jargon wherever possible. They are often prone to fashion and outmoded phrases will make you look outdated. Long complicated sentences don't work either. They do not display how clever you are, they merely trip the eye, confuse the reader and make your letter harder to read.

Blaise Pascal said, 'I have made this letter longer than usual, only because I have not had the time to make it shorter' (*Lettres provinciales* 16, 1665). He understood that to write in plain, clear terms is actually not always very easy. Don't be afraid to draft an important letter out, set it aside for a time, then read it afresh and edit it. At the same time, try not to overwork it. It will lose its spontaneity.

So, be yourself and tell it as it is. But whatever you do, never fail to write that letter!

Chapter summary

- Consider the presentation of your letter
- Think about your choice of writing paper and envelopes
- Decide the best way to lay out your letter
- Take care with greetings and sign-off, and the appropriate titles or forms of address
- Avoid pretentious style, dated slang and jargon – keep it simple

2
Netiquette

2.1 EMAIL: THE PROS AND CONS

Email is exciting, simple and fun to use. It's immediate and succinct – the perfect way to communicate in the 21st century.

Or is it? Basically email is just another method of communication, an alternative to fax, phone or post, but considerably quicker. It permits you at the click of a mouse to send a single line, or many lengthy documents as attachments. It is indeed a marvel, and at its best can save hours of working time, allowing the easy and instant transmission of information to one person or a number of people. Its other great advantage is for people with business contacts, friends or relations in other countries: it gives convenient access across international time zones. You can have a flow of emailed 'conversation' without having to telephone early, late or in the middle of the night.

What it has also become – not always to our advantage – is a genre all of its own, and some of the developments have a high irritant factor. It's the content and the way it is presented that often becomes problematic. Managing and filing emails can also waste time and create stress in many working situations. It seems that because the delivery of messages is instant, users are putting the messages together in an 'instant' format, sometimes without due thought, and they expect replies equally quickly.

Some major organizations now have guidelines to email usage and, if you work for a large company, it may be worth checking to see if such a policy document is available – or even show initiative by suggesting that one is produced. Even so, such documents cannot take the place of a common-sense attitude.

Email can be a very impersonal form of communication, possibly because of the short, snappy emailspeke, where brevity is all. There is a danger that people can use it to keep their colleagues and customers at arm's length, particularly if there is negative news around. In some offices, staff email one another across a crowded room rather than walking across to talk to one another. People are losing the ability to maintain good face-to-face relationships in the workplace, and beyond. Email facilitates a new kind of laziness.

Dr Susan Mayor, a highly qualified medical journalist, who writes for the *British Medical Journal* and other prestigious healthcare publications, says this: 'I have more misunderstandings through emails than any other form of communication. Brevity often comes over as rudeness and I've been hurt, even in a professional capacity, by terse comments. But when I have explained this to the sender, they have been devastated. They hadn't realized how they came over.'

A young publisher explains: 'I use email when I want to pull out of an invitation or a meeting. It's easier than having to explain in person on the phone, easier on me anyway. At the same time, I do want to be a better networker, but I dread having to meet new people. I'm not good at chatting. I suppose, because we're using email and texting all the time, we're getting out of the habit of talking to other people properly.'

Setting the problems of spam (electronic junk mail) aside, there are many elements of email management and courtesies which can be established and will improve the kind of communications we currently send. Interestingly, most of the guidelines below have originated as a response to poor practice, rather than being the result of considered thinking about how to use this wonderful new communication tool.

2.2 CLEAR SUBJECT LINE

It's one of the starting points and requires care and consideration. Having an appropriate subject or title line sounds obvious, yet this is one area that many people find a problem. For instance, there are emailers who use a title they consider to be appealing, cute or funny. Unfortunately, the title may not be considered sensible by the recipient and therefore the email is deleted unread. Another error is to use a subject line that is so unspecific as to be unrecognizable for its subject matter a week or so later. Subject lines such as 'Yesterday's meeting' or 'Progress Report' won't mean much by the following week. Other subject lines of dubious value are: 'Thank you', 'Hi', 'Update' and 'How is it going?'

And then there are the sinners who use no subject line at all. Be aware that some recipients (including the author) will automatically bin any email without a subject, presuming it to be spam.

Other people will use the reply mechanism again and again. This is fine if there is a stream of correspondence about just one topic. Problems start when, along the way, other entirely different topics are introduced, but the old subject or title line is still being used. This may result in new topics becoming 'lost', and possibly important information becoming untraceable later on.

If you are introducing a different subject, pick a new and appropriate title for it.

2.3 COPYING OTHERS

This too requires consideration of what is appropriate. Does the main recipient need to know who else is receiving this? Sometimes it may be very important to that recipient that he or she knows who else is privy to the communication. In other cases, you may wish to advise a person of your correspondence with someone else, without that someone knowing. In this instance, you will want to send the copy blind (usually listed in the address boxes as bcc).

If you have a number of people with whom you wish to share sight of the correspondence, do you wish each of those people to see the email addresses of all the others copied in? In some instances, there may even be a privacy issue in doing so. For example, if you are copying the email to people who are very important or who have given you their email address on a confidential basis, will they feel that you have breached their security or broken faith by 'advertising' their address to the others copied in?

Another example: let's suppose that you are a freelance practitioner or small business and you wish to circulate some information to all your clients. Are you sure that they will not mind their email addresses being seen by the others? Do you really wish one client to know who your other clients are?

Some people find it irritating to be copied in at a late stage on a stream of emails. It means that they have to scroll through trying to pick up the threads of the problem, topic or issue. Sometimes this cannot be helped, but it may be courteous to add your apologies for the amount of reading involved.

2.4 INFORMATION OVERLOAD

A related – and fairly major – issue is that of information overload. We all know about this. Some of us dread seeing the number of emails awaiting us after even the shortest break or holiday. It is highly irritating that, even after deleting the junk, so many communications, often those marked 'for information', are not really relevant.

Theresa Britt of the Open University quotes ruefully the following example: 'We have 4,000 people in buildings across our Walton Hall campus at Milton Keynes, and thousands more in regional offices. We therefore have not only our external emails coming in, but those from an extensive internal system. The problem comes when emails for people in a particular department at Walton Hall are sent to all the members of that department, some of whom are based in, say, Dublin or Leeds. Sometimes I receive an email telling me that there are some sandwiches left over from a presentation lunch on the third floor of another Walton Hall building, all because someone pressed the Copy All button. I receive several hundred emails after a few days away. I certainly don't need these time-wasters as well.'

The message is, when in doubt, you probably don't need to copy everyone unless they *really* need the information.

2.5 RECEIPTS

Some people don't mind a request to send a receipt; others find them a nuisance. There are still people who have a dial-up email connection and so sending for a receipt is not a simple press of a button but a separate procedure.

The Sent box will tell you if an email has been sent successfully. If it hasn't arrived, it will have bounced back. Admittedly this cannot tell you if your email has been read and fully appreciated. If it is essential that you know when your communication has been read, you may indeed have to ask for a receipt; otherwise it may be more polite to assume that the email has received attention.

2.6 **ATTACHMENTS**

Be aware that not everyone has broadband or a computer system that will accept large files easily. For instance, many independent practitioners use a single PC or Mac of a domestic size, and may still be on a dial-up connection. If you were to send massive attachments, you could be blocking their system for hours. The same applies if you wish to send video clips or email your favourite holiday photos to all your chums. In this instance, the solution would be to check with your webmail provider. Some of these now provide a free service for sharing photos; you simply register with them, create an online photo album and send the link, with a password, to your friends.

If you are not sure whether someone can receive a large attachment easily, it is courteous to send a text email first, advising the attachment size you wish to send. They can then let you know if it is not acceptable. Ali Musa who runs MacMedicine suggests that no attachment should exceed 100kb without prior consultation.

For this reason, be aware that sending jokey graphics, animation, elegant backgrounds and other irrelevances may also completely disturb someone else's working schedule because they take so long to come through. In fact, for most people, a few large attachments will fill the email account.

2.7 SALUTATIONS AND SIGN-OFF

In polling friends, colleagues and clients, I discovered that of all the irritants about emails, the lack of a salutation gained by far the highest score. It's not a generational thing either. Younger as well as older people find it downright rude if you do not use some kind of salutation. It can be 'Hi, Susan' or 'Hello, Jim', rather than 'Dear Mr Jones', but the hi, hello or dear are considered essential for politeness. Generally, it is considered far too abrupt if you do not use a salutation.

Equally disliked was the use of someone's name on its own, when there is no other salutation. Most people feel that starting an email with only the recipient's name – 'Sam' or 'Jill' – sounds as though a very brusque order is to follow.

Signing off an email doesn't seem to bring quite so much heated debate. Even so, people said that they preferred some kind of farewell. It can range from 'best wishes' to 'cheers' or even 'thanks'. Here, it is the thought that counts.

Many expressed the wish for a signature line which gave an alternative contact, perhaps a phone number. That way, the recipient has the option to call you if their email is down at some future point, or merely to hear your voice and have a real-life conversation.

2.8 ABBREVIATIONS AND TEXT SPEKE (AND SHOUTING)

They are cute and can be fun. They are modern and show that you are at the cutting edge. It may also be that the use of abbreviations is yet another irritating development. How can this be? Again, consider who will be receiving your email. It's easy to slip into the habit of using abbreviations but you may cause misunderstandings, if not immediately, then at some future time.

Are your abbreviations really:

- *Time saving?* It's fine if the person you are emailing is from the same profession, social group and culture. However, most trades and professions develop their own vernacular and, if you add in a few abbreviations as well, the email becomes impenetrable to everyone else outside that circle. In the same way, social groups tend to develop a certain 'speke'. This too can exclude anyone who does not belong to that group. The time people spend trying to understand your email is wasted time for them and, if you repeat the offence, may jeopardize your relationship with them.

- *Understandable?* If English is not your recipient's first language, they may spend time trying to understand your abbreviations and may well come up with some entirely different explanations. Even within the UK, some abbreviations have alternative meanings. For example, LoL can be Loads of Laughs, Laugh out Loud or, equally, it can be Lots of Love. Such interpretations may not be interchangeable.

- *Appropriate?* What a difference a year makes. What is new, fresh and amusing now is boring, tired and dated within a year. If your email is sufficiently important to be kept on file, it is possible that abbreviations may be inappropriate or even down-right embarrassing at some future point.

Another development of text speke is to avoid the use of any capital letters or punctuation. It may be a quick way for someone to write an email but it may infuriate the recipient. Quite a few of the people I have spoken to about this chapter objected to the time they waste deciphering an email which has no punctuation and is totally in lower case. It can work as a text message but emails tend to look more like the printed page and we are not used to seeing uncapitalized and unpunctuated print. Again, it is a question of what your recipient will find acceptable.

AND then there's the use of capital letters. In current usage, any word appearing in capitals is deemed as a SHOUT. Sometimes that may be totally fitting ('We've just heard: we have WON the account!', 'It's a BOY!', 'We've got the house. HURRAY!'). In more general, less dramatic situations, it may come across as too strong or even aggressive.

2.9 PRIORITY AND SWIFT RESPONSE

Everyone has pet hates. For Steven Dowling at the National Confidential Enquiry into Patient Outcome and Death, one of the major health audits, it's the over-use of the Priority button. He finds that an increasing number of emailers mark their emails as 'High Importance' in order to gain immediate attention. Frequently, the emails are not high priority, and so the Priority button loses its impact.

It's also easy to fall into the trap of believing that because email is so immediate the response will be equally swift. If you start to feel irritated that someone has not replied to you quickly, ask yourself if *you* are always plugged in to your computer or mobile. It's possible that you may like to move away from your desk, go to meetings, take uninterrupted time over lunch, go on holiday ... or just talk to other human beings face-to-face for a time, without having to check the ether every ten minutes. So, if that applies to you, remember that the person you have just emailed might feel the same.

2.10 LEGALITY

Nowadays, emails are considered legal documents in many countries. Agreements made via emails will be legally binding, and copies of emails will be considered legal documents, acceptable in court.

If you are making an agreement of any kind, or an order for goods or services, take care with your wording and if necessary seek professional advice. Similarly, if you are accepting an order or commission, take responsibility for the agreement and ensure that every aspect is considered and covered, just as you would if it were in a hard-copy form.

There are other legal implications. You must not circulate any copyrighted or licensed materials via email, even though they may not originate with you. In the same way, do not use someone else's identity or passwords in order to gain access to their emails. Some organizations take this so seriously that you could be fired for this misrepresentation and invasion of privacy. Do not give out your password or user ID.

Finally, don't send on chain letters through the Internet.

2.11 SCATTERED THINKING

There was a time when people sat down and worked out a full order or brief for a project, then handed it, faxed it or posted it to the person or team who would be responsible for its execution. Email has sometimes eroded this good business practice. Many service departments, suppliers and freelance practitioners complain of the 'scattered thinking' approach which is becoming more and more prevalent.

A rough order or brief arrives, to be followed day by day, sometimes even hour by hour, by additional thoughts, theories and instructions. These 'Oh, by the ways' can make a job unnecessarily complicated. This practice wastes time and can lead to any number of misunderstandings.

Andie Airfix at Satori, graphic designer for the rock

music industry, automatically prints out every email he receives relating to the commission in hand. He finds that, even before he has started on the project, he has a small file of instructions, some of which are contradictory. He then draws up a draft brief, emails it to everyone concerned and asks for clarification. Only then will he proceed.

2.12 FILING AND HARD COPIES

Life can be easier if you have a tidy desk space – and a neat email account. Here are some tips which may help you:

- Delete all junk mail immediately.
- Delete all the items in your Deleted Mail folder.
- Delete all the items in the Sent Mail folder – or transfer them to personal folders (see below).
- Set up personal folders and move any email you wish to retain into them. Back them up now and again if they contain valuable information that you don't have stored safely elsewhere.
- As suggested earlier, it helps considerably if you use pertinent subject titles. If necessary, number your files or show the date as part of the subject.
- Where appropriate, also keep a hard copy in a separate file. Remember, these can also act as legal documents.

2.13 GOOD EMAIL WRITING

Take time to get it right, as you would with any other form of communication. The key words are brevity, clarity and courtesy. Give your email a strong title, easy to identify later on, relevant to the subject matter. Ensure that it only goes to those who need to know. Consider whether anyone copied in should be copied visibly or 'blind'. Make a polite salutation and an equally polite sign-off, with your full name and telephone contact showing underneath.

If you are writing to someone who will read your email on a computer, you can afford to be wordier. If someone is likely to be picking their emails up via their mobile phone, you may wish to be more succinct.

2.14 EXPERT ADVICE

Ali Musa of MacMedicine, which provides specialist Mac consultancy and training for creatives such as photographers, designers and artists, says:

There are all kinds of new Internet communication gaining in popularity, for example Skype, which is just around the corner as mainstream technology and will allow people to make international calls for free. Even then, email will still be needed to send fast messages or files across time zones, or for when people aren't available in person, and of course for written confirmation. It is therefore well worthwhile learning to use email in an efficient, polite and appropriate way.

Take time to read your emails properly. Don't be so quick to hit the Send button. Does the text make sense, not only to you but to the recipient? Is the tone appropriate to the person you are sending it to? Is the salutation too formal or too friendly? Does the subject line encapsulate what the email is about? A good subject line will bear fruit when you search through your emails later on. If you want to copy someone else in, should the main recipient know? If you are copying lots of people in, do you really want to circulate all those addresses to everyone on the list, or should you be sending it 'blind'? A well-formed email will save you time in the long run and avoid crossed wires (and cross clients).

Nick Elliott is director of international business at Romeike International, the media monitoring and evaluation company. Romeike has 2,500 staff globally, 350 of whom are in the UK, with about 200 in the London headquarters.

Email is great for document sharing and confirming meeting notes; it's very useful on a practical level. However, I have found it never resolves problems. I realized that it was leading to a breakdown of office communications here, even within a 50 metre radius, because people were emailing one another rather than talking.

There were so many stupid misunderstandings on the yes-I-did, no-you-didn't level. People could not see one another, they couldn't hear the voice tone or see the body language, which is how we know if someone really is cross, and so they inevitably took offence at these clipped email messages. Then we would get emails being copied across to me, a sort of sneaking to the boss. A lot of stubbornness crept in.

So I pulled the whole team together and explained that I was banning inter-office emailing. I used examples but didn't assign blame. The ban started among forty or so staff and then spread through other parts of the group. As a result we now have a much happier ship. If people have an issue, they get up and go and talk to one another. If necessary, they bring the problem to me. But, either way, the matter is resolved much quicker, in a matter of minutes. On email, resentment would build up and issues would drag on for days.

Another irritating practice is when people copy you in as a quick way of keeping you in the loop. If you are managing a large team, maybe thirty or forty people, you simply don't have time to read all the copies. What you really need is a proper report.

I also encourage everyone to add their phone number to their email sign off. I may wish to talk to you! If you don't include the phone number, you are keeping me at arm's length. You can use email for the nuts and bolts, but relationships with colleagues and clients are built up by conversation.

Chapter summary

- Take *time* and put thought into writing and responding to emails
- Give each email an appropriate title or subject line
- Only copy in when necessary and be aware of privacy issues in divulging email addresses to others
- Beware of creating information overload
- Give a salutation – it's polite – and include your telephone number in the sign-off
- Avoid abbreviations and text-speke
- Keep your filing up-to-date

3
Job Applications

3.1 STAND OUT FROM THE CROWD

We all want to get job applications right; our liveli-
hoods depend on them. We also know the chances are
that there will be lots of similar – perfectly crafted –
applications, and ours must therefore be outstanding.
Usually the initial application is in two parts: your
curriculum vitae (CV or career history, also sometimes
called a résumé) and a covering letter.

There are three main types of application:

- *reply to a job advertisement*, usually a letter with a
  copy of your CV attached, or increasingly these days,
  an online application.
- *approach to a head-hunter or appointments agent*,
  enquiring about the kinds of jobs currently on offer,
  usually including a copy of your CV.
- *speculative application to a company or organization*,
  not currently advertising, but for whom you would
  be interested to work. (You would not normally send
  a CV with these sorts of applications.)

In all three instances, you will wish to make your presentation attractive, which will probably mean crisp and modern, with the emphasis on clarity. Ensure that you structure it so that it is easy to read. If it is difficult, you will be making the reader work hard to understand and interpret it and they may then not bother.

3.2 THE IMPORTANCE OF THE COVERING LETTER

As Claire Thomas, HR manager for Penguin UK, points out, the covering letter is your main marketing tool, the part of your presentation that can make or break your interview chances. By and large, your CV is a statement of fact and, without any explanation, you are leaving the recruiter to spot any useful connections or interpret any career gaps. Few people have a smooth, uninterrupted career path. Nowadays, people have lots of choices, and opportunities to try different kinds of work, as well as to travel. If you wish, it is appropriate to use your covering letter to explain these career changes and diversions and present them in a positive light.

3.3 PRESENTATION OF LETTERS

Handwritten covering letters are acceptable where the handwriting is easy to read, although most will be written on a computer. Knowing that people are busy and may be faced with a pile of applications, consider selecting a typeface that is clear, maybe 12 or 13 point size, and set the margins wide.

Always show your address, email address and daytime

phone number. It can be on the right-hand side or centred at the top of the page. Decide if coloured notepaper is suitable. Anything too wacky – unless you are applying for a wildly creative job – may even be an irritant and be rejected out of hand. When in doubt, opt for white, cream or ivory.

3.4 THE CV

Your curriculum vitae is your career history. It is also your career 'advertisement' and, while remaining concise, it should accurately reflect the scope of your talents and achievements. At the same time, even though a CV is principally fact-based, you may wish to tailor it to each job application you make. There may be aspects which you will want to highlight as being particularly relevant to a specific role or company.

Most CVs are on one side of – usually – two A4 sheets. If you have exceptional experience, this could just run to three. They should always be typed, using a crisp easy-to-read typeface. Italics and zany or gothic scripts may be fun for personal use, but they are not appropriate for CVs, unless you are applying for a design role.

Give your biographical details: full names, address, email address, daytime phone number(s). Under a heading such as 'Personal Details', you can give your date of birth, nationality and marital status – but only if you wish to do so – and, if you are applying for a job where driving is involved, mention whether you hold a clean driving licence. These details might be given, appropriately laid out, at the top of the CV, or split between the top – showing your contacts – and end – giving the personal information.

Some people like to start with a 'Summary' or 'Personal Profile', showing succinctly in one or two paragraphs the experience they are offering, along with a statement relating to their character and attitude to work.

Example of a Summary

I am a hard worker with good communication skills and work well under pressure. I am a team player but also work effectively with minimum supervision. Possessing a good sense of humour and thriving on challenge, I can provide a helpful attitude with strong innovative and creative ideas.

I am proficient in Microsoft Office and am familiar with such programs as Word, Excel, Power Point and Outlook. I frequently use the Internet and can navigate most browsers. I am a quick learner and eager for any type of training in order to work to the best of my ability and be a real asset to any company I work for.

[reproduced with kind permission of Verity Appointments]

Follow this with a résumé of your employment, starting with the most recent. It may be appropriate to give your job title, then a few lines showing what responsibilities that job entailed. An alternative layout would be to have a job summary, with a few lines outlining the role, followed by a heading 'Achievements' which are bulleted.

Wherever possible, show how you have added to the momentum of the organizations or companies for whom you have worked, but again, keep it succinct.

However, if you have been a member of an award-winning team, or have helped a company build its turnover or win its first overseas contract, say so.

Many people experience career breaks for various reasons and it is wise to list these too. For example,

2000–2001   *Career break to permit caring for elderly relative*

or

2000   *Sabbatical to enable me to undertake life-long ambition to sail around the world/write a book/support my partner through the early stages of our twin daughters' babyhood*

After completing your employment record, you may wish to add those 'extras' which might impress a potential employer. You may have studied for additional qualifications, or belonged to relevant professional organizations, or undertaken voluntary work which has given you experience appropriate to the job you are applying for. You can list such factors under a separate heading, such as 'Additional Information'. Information about your schooling and further education is probably appropriate at this point.

Finally add your interests. Though this should not be a long section, it shows that you are a rounded human being if you belong to sports or social clubs, play a part in community affairs, belong to a band or run in the London Marathon for charity.

There are software programs which offer a CV 'wizard' but these look formulaic and potential employers will be able to spot them quickly. By all means use them as a template or aide memoire but it might be better to use your own design and let your individuality shine through.

Every employer and prospective employee has a different opinion of how a perfect CV should look. Ultimately you will want something with which you feel comfortable – and proud.

Example of a CV

David Keily, 73 Grosvenor Road, London E. ...
Home telephone: 020 8444 0001
Mobile: 06892 123457
Nationality: British
Date of Birth: 12 November 1965 (optional)

I am a self-confident individual who has the ability to work well on my own or as part of a team. I thrive under pressure and I am used to working to deadlines and meeting targets. I possess excellent communication skills both written and verbal, and I am confident dealing with members of the public either in person or on the telephone. Over the past 18 months I have also gained valuable managerial and team leader experience.

Career to Date:

2000–present   Senior Practice Manager of Southwold NHS Primary Care Trust

– full partner of practice, which has four GPs, a physiotherapy unit, community nursing and wellness clinics
– In the past two years I have developed a practice strategy

*which takes into account the deprivation issues encountered
in the catchment area*
*– responsibilities include HR, continuing professional devel-
opment training for staff, procurement of equipment and
additional services, maintaining patient records, and general
administration.*

1996–2000   Practice Manager of Northwood NHS Primary
Care Group

*– involvement in the setting up of Northwood as a PCG, and
preparing for its trust status*
*– learning the skills required in managing a primary care
team and the requirements of and pressures on clinicians as
well as administrators*
*– handling enquiries from patients attending the practices
and clinics*
– deputizing for Senior Practice Manager during holiday times

1991–1996   Assistant Practice Manager of Eastling Medical Centre

– learning my skills in this busy multi-cultural centre

1987–1991   Administration Assistant, Records Office,
Westward District Hospital

*– an introduction to audit of hospital records, the introduc-
tion of supplying information to central agencies and the
national confidential enquiries, and the liaison between
hospitals and primary care centres*
*– setting up and standardizing procedures of computerized
records for patients*

1986–1987   Gap year, spent travelling, following university

Education:

2002–2003   The Open University: Diploma in Systems Management

1983–1986   University of Central Studies: 2.1 degree in Business Management

Wapping Grammar School: 3 A Levels   8 GCSEs

Other Information:

Following my success in gaining my Diploma through the Open University, I have now joined a learning set with individuals from other market sectors which has proved invaluable in the development of my leadership skills. I have also run in the Flora London Marathon to raise funds for the World Wildlife Fund.

3.5 RESPONDING TO AN ADVERTISEMENT

Always start your covering letter by stating the job for which you are applying (the company may be advertising for several kinds of staff at the same time) and giving the date and publication, or the place, in which the advert appeared. For example:

Dear Sir,

I am writing in response to your advertisement in the Surrey Advertiser on 30th January for a sales executive in your Spare Parts Department.

or

Dear Sir,

I am writing in response to your advertisement in the Job
Centre for a catering manager.

or even

Dear Sir,

A friend who works for your company has informed me that
you have a vacancy in your administration department and
I would like to be considered.

If there is a job reference number included in the advert,
don't forget to quote it at the top of your letter. It helps
the recipient and it also shows your attention to detail.

In smaller companies, it may be the chief executive
or managing director who makes the first (and final)
selection. If you are applying for a job in a large company or organization, it's more than likely that the
Human Resources (HR) department will be filtering
the replies, evaluating the applications, and making
the first selection for interview, on behalf of the line
manager in the department of the company requiring
the staff. Recruitment is only one small (albeit important) part of the function of HR departments. Very
large HR departments may have personnel dedicated
only to recruitment, but even so, these are busy people.
This helps you to set the tone of your letter.

It will be appreciated if you reflect what is in the
advertisement, and it will make your chances of selec-

tion for interview more likely. It shows that you, as the applicant, have thought about the job and made the decision that your skills and experience would be relevant. Study the words they have used. Try to judge as accurately as possible what skills and personal qualities the advertiser is looking for. You will then be able to decide what parts of your career record and personality are a match, and which traits you will wish to emphasize.

Some large organizations add a strapline or a mission statement, describing their business, in their advertisement. If they do, you may wish to refer to that information. For example:

Advert:
'Blythe & Brown: offering healthcare solutions throughout the world.'

You might wish to say in your letter that your ambition is to work for a UK-based company which is at the forefront of global biotechnology. Another example:

Advert:
'The country's leading charity for animal welfare.'

You might write: *I have always wanted to work in the voluntary sector and the welfare of animals is very close to my heart.*

Check the company's web site. If possible, find a way to show that you have taken the trouble to research something about the organization you are applying to, perhaps relevant to its mission, products or financial performance.

Some adverts will request a CV at the outset; others

will ask you to send for an application form in hard copy or to fill one in online. Either way, take your time in completing it. Make your application as relevant as possible to the job you are seeking. Be sure to include all the training and experience you have had, however trivial you think it may be, if it is appropriate to the job specification. Even hobbies or leisure pursuits that are in some way associated might help demonstrate your interest in the potential sphere of work.

If you are applying to work in a not-for-profit organization, for example, and you have worked previously as a charity volunteer, your experience is relevant and worth detailing.

Examples of responses to job adverts

Flat 3, 101 Pershore Road, Bromley KT.. ...

The HR Director
The Trading Company
London Wall
London EC. ...

4th May 20—

Dear Sir or Madam,

Personal Assistant for the Trading Company

Please would you consider me as an applicant for the position of PA in your company. I was delighted to see this vacancy as I have always wanted to work for an international agency as prestigious as yours. I know that you have clients in Eastern

Europe as well as other parts of the world, and this is of particular interest to me.

In July 2004 I graduated from the University of Latvia with a BA degree in English Philology. In addition to this formal education, I gained a merit from a course on 'An Integrated Approach to PR' from the London School of Public Relations.

Until March 31 I worked as a marketing and PR Assistant for — Bank Plc (the Latvia branch). My tasks were connected with project management, internal and external communications, translations and web design.

I am also fluent in three languages, English, German and Latvian, in addition to my mother tongue which is Russian. I am an experienced user of a wide range of computer software, and my typing speed is 50 wpm.

As an EU citizen, I am eligible to work in the UK. I am a responsible and innovative self-starter who is able to meet tight deadlines and assimilate information in a short time. I would like to improve my knowledge base and make a very real contribution to the development of your company.

References from my current and previous employers, as well as proof of my professional and educational background (my diplomas), are available at your request. My CV is enclosed.

Yours faithfully,

Victoria Berezova

First Floor, Cromwell House, The Bridleway, Bath B.. ...

Mr A Hathaway
The Antique Shop
High Street
Little Lanes
Bath B.. ...

3rd April 20—

Dear Mr Hathaway,

Manager/Sales Assistant

I was very interested to see your advertisement for a manager/
sales assistant for the Antique Shop in last night's Bath Chron-
icle, and I would like to be considered for the post. As you
will see from my attached CV, I have extensive experience in
the retail trade, both on the high street and with more specialist shops.

Although I have worked for a craft shop in the past, I
haven't had direct experience of the antiques trade. However,
antiques have been my passion since I was a child and on a
modest level I collect ceramics from the 1920s and 1930s,
and also sports memorabilia. To combine my working life with
my keenest hobby would be truly wonderful, and I have been
seeking just such an opportunity for some time. I have visited
your shop several times and always loved the atmosphere. I
do so hope you will view my application with sympathy.

Yours sincerely,

Clive Barrett

11 Belsize, The Causeway, Leamington Spa CV. ...

The HR Director
Small Appliances Manufacture Ltd
Hull H.. ...

14 November 20—

Dear Sir,

Operations Director, North West, Ref ASM.114

I am responding to your advertisement in the Daily Telegraph of 13th November for an Operations Director, and I enclose my career history. The job specification as described is a very close match to my own experience, not only in the nature of the work but also in that my career to date has been in an associated industry sector. In fact, I have interacted with your company on a number of occasions and I have always been impressed by the professionalism of its representatives.

The salary range you are quoting would represent a substantial promotion for me and I would expect to reflect that in my commitment and quality of work. I enjoy motivating a team, enhancing each member's individual talents and creating a smooth-running department. At the same time, I believe that I am a good communicator at all levels of an organization. I am available for interview at any time. I am also very happy to relocate should I be successful in my application.

Yours faithfully,

Timothy Chapman

3.6 APPROACHING AN EMPLOYMENT AGENCY

For many kinds of work there are specialist employment agencies. There are agencies specifically for lawyers, medical practitioners, nurses and care workers, secretaries and administrators, charity fundraisers, security staff, catering personnel, public relations people and so on. If you are looking for a job or contemplating a job change, you can register with the kind of appointments agency appropriate to your sphere of work.

In this instance, you will not have the guidance of a specific job advertisement, and so will be offering the widest view of your talents and background. You should state whether you are actively seeking a job or just having a scout around. You may wish to specify the kind of employer you would consider ideal:

- a local, national or international organization.
- small, medium-sized or large in terms of numbers of personnel.
- companies offering apprenticeships or in-house training programmes, or support at postgraduate or continuing professional development levels.
- organizations which offer flexible or part-time working, or have crèche or after-school clubs for employees' children.

You may also choose to specify companies or organizations that you do not want to work for. There is no need to explain why. Simply state that you do not wish your details to be forwarded to the following, then list the companies in question.

3.7 WRITING SPECULATIVELY

Lots of people have found their dream job by writing 'on spec' to the kind of companies or organizations they would like to work for. Many well-known companies keep a file of letters from would-be staff, and will refer to that file when they are recruiting, rather than spending on advertisements or hiring an appointments agency.

It is wise to be open in your admiration of the company, for example:

> Your reputation in retailing is unique and I have always enjoyed shopping in your stores. The merchandise is always of such a high quality and the staff are so helpful. I am wondering if there are any vacancies . . .

or

> I have read about the highly creative campaigns you have achieved for your clients. I have always wanted to work in your area of advertising.

Take notice of the business press, not only the job adverts but the news and feature pages. If you see an article about a company that impresses you, you could always write and say so. Don't be embarrassed about this; by and large, people thrive on compliments. An example would be:

I saw the profile of you and Porters Plc in The Times Business supplement and was hugely impressed. I was fascinated that your company only operates under fair trade agreements as I am a firm believer in ethical trading. I would love to know more about your enterprise, and wonder if there is a possibility of meeting you.

It is then up to you to decide whether to mention what your skills are and the fact that you are seeking new employment.

If you are invited for an interview, it is worth confirming that you will be attending – again this shows your attention to detail. Your letter or return email need only be very simple:

Mr I. Harris,
HR Department
The Consultancy
King Street
London W.. ...

29th April, 20—

Dear Mr Harris,

Graphic Designer for The Consultancy

Thank you for your letter of 27th April. I will be delighted to attend an interview on Friday, 6th May at 11 a.m., and I will bring a portfolio of samples of my design work to show you.

Yours sincerely,

Susan Chapman

3.8 EXPERT ADVICE

Shernaz Engineer started the appointments agency Verity in 1993 and now has more than thirty recruiters on her staff. She advises:

> Enthusiasm is what sells, so take your time, make an effort and do your research for each and every application. Don't make the mistake of using the same CV and covering letter for every application; tailor them to each advert.

Many people have much the same career experience, so try to let your personality show through. Have something that will make your application stand out from the pile.

There are certain key words and phrases that bring joy to potential employers' hearts. These include:

- I am keen to develop my career
- I am pro-active
- I persevere until the job is completed
- I have an eye for detail
- I am flexible
- I have a sense of humour
- I enjoy being a team player

This last one is very important. By and large, employers want someone who will fit in and work well with their current team, not an individual – however talented – who wanders off into la-la land or who is unable to relate to others.

Another mistake is to pretend you can do something

that in fact you cannot. However, if it is a minor requirement – knowing how to use the latest form of Excel for example – you can always rush out and brush up your skills. In order to demonstrate your initiative, you could even say something on the lines of 'the ad specifies that you require someone with basic Excel skills. Although I don't currently have knowledge of Excel, I have booked myself on a course next week to learn Excel.'

Chapter summary

- Research the company or organization you are applying to
- Tailor your CV and covering letter to each job advertisement
- Emphasize where your skills and experience are appropriate to each application
- Make your covering letter easy to read and give all your contact details
- Be enthusiastic, honest and open
- If you are asked for an interview, confirm you will attend in writing

4

References, Resignations and Retirement

REFERENCES

On occasions we are required to present – or to write – references. The most usual kind are either job references or those requested when we take on a letting property or we let a property ourselves.

If you are proposing to give someone's name as a referee, it is courteous to ask them first, and then later to write and thank them, and let them know the outcome.

4.1 JOB REFERENCES

Increased employment legislation over the last few years has meant that employer references are increasingly based on statements of fact, and not personal opinions, which may be biased and discriminatory. Generally, all the information given in a reference should be based on fact or capable of independent verification.

Some people question the value of job references

since there are such strict regulations relating to what can and cannot be expressed. But the Chartered Institute of Personnel and Development (CIPD) recommends that employers should always take up references in order to check facts such as qualifications gained and previous jobs held. However, they add that they do not recommend that employers rely on subjective opinion with regard to competence or performance.

If this sounds confusing, here is an example. It would be deemed subjective if you, as an employer, said that a former employee 'is a good team player'. It would be more factual – and as effective – if you were to say that the employee was a member of a highly successful team. That the team was successful and the employee was a member of that team are both facts that can be verified.

Most employers will ask for two references. In the past, one was traditionally from a former employer, the other a character reference. Nowadays, both references are likely to be from current and former employers. If you are new to the job market, the references may be provided by an academic source. Usually references are only taken up when a job offer has provisionally been made.

The current employer may be legally liable if a reference includes unlawful discrimination. References must be true, accurate and fair. This also means that the reference should not be misleading. For example, according to *The Penguin Guide to Employment Rights*, if a reference claims that an employee is honest and trustworthy, but in fact he or she was dismissed for theft, then the new employer could bring a claim for any losses arising from the negligent reference.

In fact, there is no legal obligation to provide a reference to a former employee, although it's rare for an employer to refuse, because it may have a negative effect on the employee's prospects. Even so, an increasing number of organizations and companies are reluctant to provide anything other than strictly factual references. It is not uncommon to receive a reference saying, 'It is not company policy to provide references. I can however confirm that X was employed by us from (date) to (date) as a (job title).' In certain circumstances, where there is a compromise agreement, for example, part of the agreement may be the provision of a reference agreed by both sides.

The information which can legitimately be sought is a factual check on the employee's:

- employment history
- job title
- qualifications and experience
- length of service
- any achievements, career development or specific identified problems
- honesty
- timekeeping
- reason for leaving

Many organizations now use forms with 'tick boxes'. Other reference requests might be less constrained and along the lines of 'give us an indication of (applicant's name) reliability, honesty, ability to work with others and any other information which you feel might influence our decision as to his/her employment'. However, this leads us into the realms of subjectivity again.

Another area for caution is that data relating to the health record of the applicant might contravene the Data Protection Act 1998. The CIPD states: 'Disclosing information relating solely to the number of days of absence will not amount to the processing of sensitive personal data. However, more detailed information which is held about workers' physical or mental health may amount to the processing of sensitive personal data . . .' Where an employee has a high level of sickness absence, the figures by themselves may create an unfair impression. In this instance, the applicant may wish to explain or identify absences that were due to hospitalization or other causes.

4.2 EXPERT ADVICE

Claire Thomas is HR Manager for Penguin UK. She says:

The important thing is that you must be consistent in giving references so that you are fair to all employees. For example, if your policy is not to provide references, other than to confirm dates of employment, this should be applied to all reference requests, however excellent the applicant. In this situation, if a manager wishes to provide a more comprehensive reference, they can write a personal reference for the individual which is not written on behalf of the company.

Sometimes we do receive a poor reference. We had one recently which raised a specific issue about a new recruit. We chose to do nothing about this but were obviously mindful of the comment. We have a probationary period anyway. But naturally any employer will be nervous if they receive a bad reference.

If a potential employee is, let's say, disruptive in some way, we can usually pick this up from the reference, not from what is said but from what is omitted.

The reference form, with tick boxes, means that you have more control over the information that you receive back as you are directing the referees' attention to key areas and it's very obvious if they are avoiding answering any questions! However, many still require the referee to make a subjective judgement so I'm sure these will be refined soon to cover only factual information.

Even so, when you give a reference, it's very important that you don't see it as just another form to fill in, another report to write. You are dealing with someone's life and you could change its course. Think about the kind of reference you would like to have written about you, the courtesy which you would wish to be shown.

Example of a reference request
The cover letter to the reference form would normally say:

Maple and Oaktree Ltd, The Grove, Maplethorpe ML.. ...

Mrs Watson
Chief Executive
The Furniture Makers
Guildford GU.. ...

29 July 20 —

Dear Mrs Watson,

Re: Mavis Allsop

The above named person has been offered the position of [job title] at [name of company] and has given your name as a referee.

I would be very grateful if you could complete and return the enclosed reference form at your earliest convenience.

All information will be treated in the strictest confidence and without any liability on your part.

Yours sincerely,

Henry Higgins
Human Resources Manager

Typical questions on a reference form would be:

Dates employed:
Job title:
Salary at date of leaving: [although this is now used less for fear of breaching the Data Protection Act]
Reason for leaving:
Number of days' absence:

Then, the tick box questions:

	Excellent	Good	Fair	Poor
Punctuality				
Honesty/Integrity				
Quality of work				
Relationships with colleagues				

The cover letter to the completed reference form might say:

Henry Higgins
Human Resources Manager
Maple and Oaktree Ltd
The Grove, Maplethorpe ML.. ...

23rd July 20—

Dear Mr Higgins,

Re: Mavis Allsop

Thank you for your enquiry about Mrs Allsop. I enclose the completed form. We are sorry to lose Mrs Allsop but understand that she must progress in her career. May I also add that I would have no hesitation in employing Mrs Allsop again here at any time.

Yours sincerely,

Mrs Watson
Chief Executive

4.3 LETTING PROPERTY REFERENCES

When you take on a letting property, the landlord or estate agent will require references from you. The better estate agents, such as Chard in south-west London, require no fewer than four: a bank reference, an employee reference, a character reference and, according to Victoria Crawford, Chard's client services manager, the most important of all, a reference from a previous landlord. As she points out, a landlord's first priority is that the new tenant will pay properly and on time. Some landlords will specify the kind of tenant they require, such as single professional people, rather than families or 'sharers', and they may also request no smokers or pets.

'A good well-written reference gives a landlord confidence,' Victoria Crawford says. 'They will be reassured if they think the tenant will report quickly if there's a small problem in the building, such as a leak, rather than leaving it until there is a major problem. And that, when they leave, the property will be in good order. It's written into the lease, of course, but often we don't have time to check before the tenant leaves.'

Example of a character reference

Victoria Court, Parkway, York

29 October 20—

Dear Mr Crisp,

I have known Mrs Janet Brown for twenty-five years. It was at first a professional relationship; she was a school teacher as was I.

The bulk of those years has seen a special relationship develop between the two of us and her family, and I would have no hesitation in offering a reference for her.

Mrs Brown is a respected member of her community through her committed work in a primary school within a socially deprived area. As a professional she has always upheld the highest standards, and I know her to be conscientious and an excellent communicator with a strong social conscience.

As a friend I know her to be loyal, responsible, honest and faithful. Mrs Brown is in a strong financial position, and her living standards are very high. Her property in York is of outstanding beauty and cleanliness.

I do not hesitate in offering this character reference.

Yours sincerely,

Mrs Jane Antrobus

Example of an employer reference

13 October 20—   Hatcher, Maythorpe & Belling
                                  River Bank, London EC. ...

Dear Sir,

Re: Miss Helen Wainwright

I confirm that Miss Wainwright has been in full employment
with this company since May 1999. She is currently employed
in our Capital Markets Division as a vice president.

We have no reason to believe that Miss Wainwright is other
than an honest and responsible person.

In accordance with company policy, this information is
given in strict confidence and without legal responsibility.

Yours faithfully,

Glenda Allen
Human Resources

Example of a landlord reference

14 April 20—

Dear Sir,

The tenants in question have been resident with us since
November 2002. During their tenancy they have been responsible and quiet and the rent has been paid promptly. They
have also kept the property in good order. I would have no

hesitation in recommending Jo and Sandy Black as tenants elsewhere.

Yours faithfully,

Malcolm Reynolds

RESIGNATIONS

The time has come to leave. Maybe you have found another job, or you may be taking time out to review your life and career.

You are not required to explain the reasons for leaving, although most bosses will ask for an explanation, if only to confirm that there aren't any problems or issues that they are not aware of. It may be that you have gained a better paid, more elevated job or you and your family are moving to another part of the country. In this instance, you may be sorry to be leaving your current employment. If you have enjoyed working for the organization and feel you have learned and benefited from employment there, it does no harm to say so. You may have the opportunity to work for them again at some future point, or with former bosses or colleagues who may themselves move on to new posts in different companies.

People sometimes seize up at writing this kind of letter and worry about the correct terminology. In fact, there is no need to resort to flowery, legalistic language in your letter. You do not have to 'tender' your resignation, or 'hereby' give notice. You can keep it very simple and write: 'I wish to resign from my post as (job title), and give you the required one month's notice.'

The company will probably acknowledge the resignation, either by letter or email, which also fulfils the legal requirement.

Examples of a resignation letter

The Crescent
Knotty Ash
L.. ...

5th November 20—

Mr Klein
HR Manager
The Organization
Liverpool L.. ...

Dear Mr Klein,

I wish to resign from my post as deputy accounts manager from today's date, and therefore give you one month's notice. I have been offered the position of accounts manager for a company in the South East, and I look forward to the greater responsibility.

May I say how much I have enjoyed working for The Organization over the last eight years, and I have benefited greatly from the training the company has invested in me. I would like to take this opportunity of thanking you and the directors for a very valuable and enjoyable period of my career.

Yours sincerely,

Henry Brown

Windway Road,
Worthing,
BN .. 2 ...

24th May 20—

Mr Bob Frank,
Chief Executive,
The Company,
80, The Street,
London, EC. ...

Dear Bob,

I am writing to resign my post with the Company and wanted to tell you personally although my line directors already know.

I have accepted a post with the University of — as Head of Collaborative Programmes. This is a new post that is focused on development of mutually advantageous initiatives with FE, business and other educational organizations, so very much up my street. I have recently moved house to Worthing, so the opportunity to work locally is very welcome.

You will remember that I transferred to the Company from the Leadership Centre with the intention of bringing the appropriate programmes and communities into a new home with potential for expansion. I began my role in the Company in May 2002 so was privileged to be able to contribute to much of the early planning and consultation for it.

I hope that I will be able to keep in touch with the Company and maybe contribute from time to time to developments. Thank you for including me in the initial developments and I wish the Company a big, bright future that will bring great benefits.

Yours sincerely,

Viv Martin,

Dr Vivien Martin
Head of Strategic Initiatives

[reproduced with the kind permission of Dr Vivien Martin]

RETIREMENT AND APPRECIATION

When someone has invested a major part of their time, their energy, talents, hopes, dreams and adult life in a job, career, or paid activity, they rightly expect due acknowledgement of their contribution when they retire. Some organizations have parties, with presents and speeches, and with current and former colleagues attending. In very large organizations, perhaps there will also be a letter from the chief executive officer or chairman. These letters may well become keepsakes for the recipient; proof that he or she had a worthwhile and successful career, something they can show their children and grandchildren.

For this reason, writing such letters should never be routine. There may be a basic formula in large organizations – a guide letter – but each one should be personalized as much as possible. This may mean a modicum of research, but spending a few minutes in this way credits the writer as well as the recipient.

Letters of appreciation are also appropriate when

someone is retiring after working in a voluntary capacity, perhaps on a committee or in an active role. Again, such letters become part of people's tributes, things they look back on in later life with pride, part of their life's achievements.

It may also be that, for a younger person, a letter of appreciation is something they can show as part of their application for another voluntary post or a paid job.

Examples of a retirement letter

Paul Scott-Lee, the Chief Constable of West Midlands Police, likes to meet as many of the officers retiring from the force as possible. Where it is not possible, he writes:

PAUL SCOTT-LEE, QPM DL   **POLICE HEADQUARTERS**
CHIEF CONSTABLE   Lloyd House
                                     PO Box 52
                                     Colmore Circus Queensway
                                     BIRMINGHAM
                                     West Midlands
                                     B4 6NQ
                                     Direct Telephone:
                                     Switchboard: (0845) 1135000
                                     Facsimile:

[Handwritten greeting]

I like to see as many as possible of the officers who are retiring on superannuation from the Force to thank them for their services and wish them well.

I very much regret that circumstances prevented my seeing you, but may I take this opportunity to express my appreciation to you for your service in the Police over the past 33 years, service which I hope you have enjoyed and found rewarding. I now have pleasure in enclosing your Commemorative Plaque and Certificate of Character, which I trust you find suitable.

Please accept my best wishes for a long and happy retirement, with the best of health to you and your family.

[Handwritten signature]

Enc

[reproduced with the kind permission of Mr Paul Scott-Lee, Chief Constable, West Midlands Police]

The Voluntary Organization, Teddington, Middx

Margaret Graham
21 Larchway Road
Kingston K.. ...

8 November 20 —

Dear Margaret

The committee has particularly asked me to thank you on their behalf for all your hard work on the committee over the past year or two.

On a personal note, I really have appreciated your helpful comments and ideas which have undoubtedly shaped events and activities.

I am sorry to hear about all your difficulties on the home

front and wish you well for the future. We certainly hope to see you at future events as and when you are able to come.

Best wishes

Linda Jones
Chair, The Voluntary Organization

Chapter summary

- A job reference must be a statement of fact and not personal opinion
- Information about an employee's health record may contravene the Data Protection Act
- Usually two references are sought from previous employers. If you are new to the job market, consider an academic source.
- Up to four references may be required for letting property: from your bank, from your employer, a character reference and from a previous landlord
- If writing to resign, you are not required to explain why you are leaving

5

Contracts and Other Business-like Letters

5.1 GET IT IN WRITING

The phrase 'get it in writing' has a very real value. By writing down what you require and what you understand any arrangements you make to be, whether they relate to business or personal affairs, you may save hassles and disasters later on. Although written contracts and agreements might appear to be just another time-consuming chore, sometimes the longest route turns out to be the quickest and most efficient. Many misunderstandings – and even outright disputes – might have been avoided had a formal order or confirmation been in place at an early stage.

Putting an agreement in writing has another benefit. Unlike a spoken agreement, a written 'brief' gives you time to reflect, to research properly, to make changes, amendments and additions, to clarify, simplify and streamline before delivering it.

Where possible, this is another instance when it is good practice to set your agreement letter to one side for at least a day, and check it again before presenting it to ensure you have covered every detail.

5.2 PERSONAL AND DOMESTIC ORDERING AND ARRANGEMENTS

If you are booking holiday accommodation or agreeing the quote for home improvements with a small company, or engaging a service such as cleaning or gardening, the onus may be on you to confirm the 'deal'. You will probably have asked for a price or quotation but, even if it has been put in writing, it is prudent to confirm that you are accepting that quote. You should also ensure that both parties know precisely what is expected of one another.

The basic rules are:

- Include your full postal address, email address (if appropriate) and daytime telephone number.
- Date your letter.
- Specify exactly the task or arrangements. Include a detailed list if necessary.
- Spell out the relevant dates and/or timescale for the work to be achieved.
- In the case of a holiday, confirm the precise length of your stay.
- Approve the amount of payment, or confirm that you are accepting the quotation.
- Confirm the method of payment, and date or dates by which it will be paid.
- If the order covers work that you, or an expert on

your behalf, wishes to inspect before completion, spell out the times or stages for those inspections.
- Don't forget to keep a copy of your letter.

If it is holiday accommodation you are booking, for example, you may wish to confirm your time of arrival, and any extras you are expecting (such as the provision of a children's cot or high chair, or a special diet).

Larger companies, such as national kitchen, bathroom or double-glazing companies, will have standard forms, letters and contracts. Even so, always check them thoroughly. If you require any variation to what has been written, you should respond as quickly as possible with a letter spelling out the omissions, additions or changes. Again, date it, and keep a copy for your own records.

If you are ordering a product, the same basic rules apply. Ask for the product by name, give any reference numbers if you know them and any other description, plus sizes, colours and, where appropriate, the materials you require. You should also specify a delivery address and any other relevant arrangements about the time of a delivery, and your preferred method of payment. This could be COD (cash on delivery) or by an invoice, or you may wish to send a cheque or banker's draft.

Examples of personal and domestic arrangements

18 Arizona Drive, Sunderland S.. ...

Mrs Sweetham
The Manager
Mount's Bay Hotel
The Cove
near Barnstaple
Devon B.. ...

30th January 20—

Dear Mrs Sweetham

Further to our telephone conversation this morning, may I confirm our requirements for one double room with bathroom en suite and a sea view, for my husband and myself, and one single room with shower, with a garden view, for our 14-year-old daughter, Amanda, for one week starting Saturday, 13th August.

We accept the tariff of £450 for the double room and £275 for the single, and understand that this covers half board, ie breakfast and evening meal. A non-returnable deposit of 20%, that is £145, is attached. We will pay the balance by debit card at the end of our stay.

We will have a long drive and don't anticipate reaching you until well into the evening on Saturday, 13th August; we will confirm an anticipated arrival nearer the date. As discussed, we also request a vegetarian and gluten-free diet for our daughter and I understand that this is not a problem.

We are very much looking forward to our stay.

Yours sincerely

Briony Grahame

Flat 2, Virgina Court, London SW.. ...

Mr Buzz Mitchell
The Flat
Notting Hill Gate
London W8 ...

12th May 20—

Dear Buzz,

Redecorating at Flat 2, Virgina Court, London SW. ...

Thank you very much for coming to see me and for your subsequent quote. I confirm that the price of £950 covering both the work and materials is acceptable. As agreed by phone yesterday, I will pay in two parts: one-third before you start the work (to cover materials) and the remaining two-thirds on successful completion of the project.

I also confirm that I would like the 'Canvas' shade, B293, for the sitting room and bedroom walls, and 'Chappell Green', B477, for the hall. All the ceilings will be white and the paintwork will be 'Canvas' eggshell.

As you know, I won't be living there while the work is underway. My phone numbers during the period – should there be any problem – are 07786 001122 and 020 7350 0000.

Yours sincerely,

Helen Wilkins

5.3 COVERING LETTERS FOR DOCUMENTS

If your accountant or solicitor has asked for some documents, it is all too easy to just slip them into an envelope and whiz them into the post. The chances are that your accountant or whoever will have lots of clients and his or her post will be opened by a secretary who may not be privy to the reason for the request. Therefore it is wise always to send a short covering letter with the documents. The same rules apply if you are faxing documents over. Ensure that your covering letter is dated and any relevant reference numbers relating to your affairs are displayed. List each of the documents. This may be immensely helpful at some future point when you want to confirm what was sent and precisely when.

If the papers are very important and you are sending them by mail, consider taking them along to the Post Office and arranging a special next-day delivery which can be signed for.

5.4 MORE FORMAL AND BUSINESS CONTRACTS

Codes of practice for work

All of the professions and most trades have umbrella organizations, part of whose remit is to produce codes of good practice. There are statutory regulations in the professions and professionals are usually aware of these. However, in other areas of work, adherence to the codes may be entirely voluntary. You may wish to find out about the code of practice relating to your sphere of work – or the work you are contracting –

and use it as a guideline for your agreement letter or contract.

Quotations, agreements and contracts

If you are arranging the contractual side of work you are doing, again check with your professional or trade organization. They may be able to help you design the necessary documents both for the quotations you need to give, and for your agreement letters.

Where possible, have these in a standard format, so you can quickly and easily personalize them to each new client or customer.

1. Quotations: Ensure that you date each one and show the name and address of the potential customer. Be exact about what the quote is for, where necessary including any relevant code numbers, quantity numbers and the precise names of the products being supplied.

If you are offering to supply goods or a service, the cost of which could rise after a given time, include a covering sentence to your quotation, such as: 'This quotation is valid for 90 days (or whatever) after which we cannot guarantee to hold these prices.'

Example of a quotation

M & M Carpet Contractors Ltd
47–48 Albert Embankment London SE1 7TN

Mr Hampson
Top Floor
79–89 Lotus Road
London SW. ...

27 June 20—
Estimate No: D07630

Dear Mr Hampson,

Further to our recent visit, we have pleasure in submitting our estimate as follows:

All carpets are supplied and fitted using a commercial felt underlay and simulated brass door plates as required.

Area: One room (9m × 4m)	Price
Quality Assured: 100% Nature wool carpet, colour to confirm	£1,120.00
To uplift and dispose of existing tiles	£ 48.00
If required to hardboard floor	£ 144.00

All prices are fully inclusive of VAT at 17.5%.
Please note that this estimate does not include any additional subfloor preparation or door adjustment (some may need planing by a carpenter), and it is valid for thirty days.
Please advise us in writing if you are aware of any pipes or cables that might be damaged during the fitting.
All areas will be assumed unfurnished to minimize costs.

A fifty per cent deposit is required on placement of order.

Assuring you of our best attention at all times.

Yours sincerely,

Malcolm Dyson
Director

[reproduced by kind permission of John Hampson and M & M Carpet Contractors Ltd]

2. *Letters of agreement:* For large-scale or on-going projects, you should consider having a written agreement or a contract with your client. This confirms legally what you have been commissioned to do and on what terms. If your customer or client does not offer a formal agreement, there's nothing to stop you from producing one which must be agreed and signed by you both. If this will be a regular requirement, you may find that it is worth consulting a solicitor who specializes in business law to help you design the letter or contract, and put together your terms and conditions.

3. *Contracts:* These will vary depending on the nature of your business and the kinds of projects you undertake.

Example of a contract

To give you some idea of what a contract letter might contain, the following is a short version of the standard consultancy/client agreement, offered as guidance to members of the Chartered Institute of Public Relations:

Address of client

Dear Client,

Agreement between

. . . . (name of practitioner)

and

. . . . (name of client)

Date . . . .

Agreement as follows:

(a) Appointment and programme
This part of the agreement confirms the appointment of the practitioner to carry out an agreed programme, the details of which can be attached.

(b) Commencement and duration
Give the dates for starting the programme and the period of duration.

(c) Fees
Detail the practitioner's service fees, exclusive of VAT, based on management, executive travelling and administration time in the UK. These will probably be listed as either an annual figure, a monthly amount or on another basis (such as a daily fee level).

This section might also point out that the practitioner reserves the right to negotiate a revised fee if the client changes its requirements.

(d) Disbursements/operating terms
This lists items which are subject to a specified handling charge. For example, the practitioner may commission other suppliers to provide goods or services, and arrange their payment themselves, recharging the client and adding a handling charge for doing so.

(e) Payment terms
This outlines how the practitioner's fees and, separately, expenses will be paid, whether it will be by cheque or an electronic bank to bank payment. The dates for payment might also be specified here.

(f) Termination provisions
This covers how the contract might be terminated by either party, the length of notice and arrangements for final payment.

(g) Trade standard terms of agreement
These appear on an accompanying document but are listed here as an integral part of the contract.

Signatures
(These are required from both parties)
For the practitioner   For the commissioner:

. . . . (name)   . . . .

. . . . (position)   . . . .

Example of 'Standard terms of agreement'
Again, every area of business will have its own requirements. Just to give you some idea of what might be covered, this is taken from the Chartered Institute of Public Relations' version:

- *Cooperation*

The client agrees to assist the practitioner by offering relevant information.

- *Exclusivity*

The practitioner will not represent conflicting interests.

- *Disbursements and expenses*

A list of those items which might apply to an agreed programme.

- *Approvals and authority*

Where written or oral agreement from the client is necessary.

- *Copyright*

Who owns what. In these days of complexity relating to intellectual property, it's as well to sort this area out in advance, rather than part-way or after the project is complete. The variations and ramifications are so complicated that, if you have any doubts, legal clarification should be sought.

- *Confidential information*

This relates to not disclosing client information without permission.

- *Insurance*

A section covering professional indemnity and the insurance issues around a client's property.

- *Disputes*

Here you would outline how there would be referral to a professional or trade institute or governing body relating to standards, in the instance of a dispute.

- *Payment in foreign currency*

List any arrangements that might be necessary.

- *Employment poaching*

This really refers to agreeing that neither the client

nor the practitioner will poach one another's staff during the duration of the contract.

• *Force majeur*

A release from contract in the event of national emergency or war.

[published with the kind permission of the Chartered Institute of Public Relations. Email: info@cipr.co.uk]

5.5 INVOICING

Keep it simple. You basically need just the date of issue, the name and address of the client or customer, a title line saying INVOICE and an invoice number. Make up a number system for yourself. Include any reference or purchase order numbers your client or customer has used in their ordering of your services or products. Then state clearly what the invoice is for. Examples might be:

• to servicing and repair on 11th March of a Jansen photocopier.
  Four hours labour
  Parts
• to a marketing and promotions service during the month of (whatever), the programme for which was agreed by you
• to the supply and delivery of 180 Halls lime green medium sized widgets, ref number: 947 ACF

List all servicing and work, and then expenses or delivery charges as separate items. In some businesses, fees might be charged on one invoice and expenses on a second. Clearly list all amounts, draw a line and give a total. If you are VAT registered, show VAT as a separate figure under the subtotal and then make a grand total. Display your VAT number at the bottom of your invoice, along with your terms for payment.

Take two copies: one for your files and one for your accounts. Post the invoice on a first class stamp.

Example of an invoice

The Perfect Plumbing Company, 8 Byways, Lincoln L. ...

Mr R. Williams
44 Allbank
Lincoln L. ...

2 February 20—

INVOICE

Invoice No: PPC 4203

To supplying and fitting Cresta 'Victoria' bath taps, bathroom sink taps and a Dimple heated towel rail

Cresta 'Victoria' bath taps, Code No CV389	£140.00
Cresta 'Victoria' sink taps, Code No CV406	£130.00
Dimple towel rail, DTR 92	£218.00
Fitting charge and labour, 2 hours @ £55	£110.00
	£598.00
VAT	£104.65
Total to pay:	**£702.65**

VAT Reg No: 4–93–84
Terms: Payment strictly within 28 days of invoice

5.6 EXPERT ADVICE

Richard Elsen is co-founder of the leading litigation and crisis public relations company, Bell Yard Communications. He adds:

All too often, disputes get out of hand because those involved have failed to agree terms at the outset. For the service provider this is usually an expensive and time consuming process that distracts them from their business and ultimately means the end of the client relationship and of course fees going forward.

The key is to write up a contract that is clear in its language and terms, or preferably use one of the template contracts that professional bodies prepare for members – and to get it signed when the business is verbally agreed.

Clarity at the outset should lead to a positive working relationship and avoid the difficulties of bitter – and lengthy – disputes which all too often involve expensive legal action and no guarantee of a win in the courts.

If problems occur you have the comfort of a written agreement, which in conjunction with firm but sensitive handling and an attitude of transparency, ought to be easier to resolve than would be the case without the necessary paperwork in place.

Perhaps more importantly, for sole practitioners and those running small companies, cash flow is extremely important – truly the life-blood of the business. A lengthy financial dispute can prove terminal to the business, or at least cause the owner (probably you!) sleepless nights worrying about whether they'll be paid – all because a simple document wasn't put forward and signed by each side at a time when goodwill is at its highest.

5.7 IF YOU HAVE CAUSE TO COMPLAIN

If you don't have a contract or agreement letter and you are not satisfied with the goods or services you have commissioned, you have several options:

- Phone or call in and see the provider and discuss your concern.
- Write and explain that you are displeased and explain precisely why. Ensure that you give dates and reference or code number for the goods or service, and explain precisely what problem has occurred and how you wish the matter to be redressed.
- Refer to any trade or professional organization to which the provider might belong.

Examples of the procedures and letters are given more fully in Chapter 10.

5.8 LATE PAYMENT AND DEBT COLLECTING

There is a great deal of stress and even anger around the area of non- or late payment. Whether it relates to a business affair or a personal loan or arrangement, it always becomes problematic when the money fails to arrive on time. Sole traders and small companies are in danger of running into cash flow problems, and personal relationships are put to the test. It's never pleasant to have to chase money.

Business payments

Some very large companies are notorious for putting their (very slow) accounting processes before the need of smaller companies and sole practitioners to be paid promptly. Thankfully, some enlightened large companies actually fast-track invoices for small concerns.

Usually, the hold-ups are with the accounts department of the company you have supplied. Fortunately, there are now all kinds of measures you can take, up to and including taking your client to court. However, this should be the very last resort. There are very useful Internet sites such as www.payontime.co.uk which explain your rights and how to enforce them.

In an ideal world, you will have avoided the problem in the first place by having a contract or agreement letter that includes payment arrangements, and your terms will be spelled out neatly at the bottom of your invoices. You may even have specified within the terms that there will be a discount for early payment, and an interest charge in the event of late payment. You will have checked on a company's creditworthiness. There are agencies who specialize in this.

If payment does not appear on time, it is advisable to send a statement immediately. Follow it up three days later with a phone call to the accounts department, and reinforce your concerns with an email or hard-copy letter to whoever commissioned you in the first place. Try to remain calm and matter-of-fact.

If you don't get a response, phone and write again, possibly in stronger tones. Point out politely that the contract or letter of agreement was very clear about terms and timing of payment. Where appropriate, ask whoever commissioned you to speak to the accounts department on your behalf. Ensure that you keep copies of all correspondence in case the situation deteriorates. If you wish to be absolutely sure that your letter has been received, trot along to the Post Office and arrange a guaranteed next-day delivery. That way, a signature has to be given by the recipient.

If your client or customer is a small company, try to discover if there is a hitch that you do not know about, such as cash flow problems at their end. This problem may not help you to get paid, but you may be able to establish when payment is likely, and make your own financial arrangements accordingly. It may be possible to arrange a part payment or instalments of payments over a period of time.

If a strongly worded letter of your own has failed to bring results, you may have to consult a solicitor if the amount in question is a large one, or consider using the County Court for smaller amounts. Nowadays, County Court proceedings are user-friendly. Local offices provide information about how to go about this, copies of forms and help with filling them in. This is where having copies of all your invoices, statements and correspondence proves so valuable.

Personal debts

This is a minefield only you can negotiate. It will depend on the closeness of your relationship with the person who owes you money, the amount concerned and the arrangements you made originally for repayment. If the relationship is valuable to you, the initial contacts about non-payment should be in person. You can then read body language as well as the tone of the other person's conversation.

If the debtor is not a friend or family member, you may wish to write in the first instance. It should be a fairly friendly letter on the lines of 'you may not have realized but the repayment is now overdue'. If there is a problem about the repayment, it helps both sides if the atmosphere is kept matter-of-fact rather than highly personal and emotional.

If you are the one who owes money

You can be sure that the problem and the debt aren't going to go away. It's probably better therefore to admit to the problem at the time – or even in advance – of the payment deadline if you know that you are unable to meet it.

Write and explain that a problem has arisen. If at all possible, explain briefly what that problem is. Where it is a temporary problem, give a timescale, and state firmly (and realistically) when you expect to be able to make payment. You can also suggest a part payment, and enclose a cheque, or ask if you can set up a schedule of instalments. If the problem is terminal, you may have to explain that too.

5.9 EXPERT ADVICE

Ann Mealor, Deputy Director of the Chartered Institute of Public Relations, says:

> Protecting your reputation – your most valuable personal as well as business asset – during a crisis is vital.

The golden rule is to communicate. Effective communications are based on honesty and transparency – and this applies just as much, if not more so, during a crisis when relationships and trust are pushed to their limits. People understand that mistakes happen and things go wrong, provided you demonstrate you can be trusted to tell the truth, to show leadership, and to act in the public interest.

This is where your long-term investment in your reputation pays off. In business, the stronger your reputation, the more leverage you have to protect the brand in a crisis. So, tell your 'stakeholders' the facts as soon as you can. It may be tempting to cover up or delay, but the truth will always out and when it does the consequences for your reputation will be significant.

Make sure your messages are consistent, internally and externally. Ensure your actions match your words and your behaviour doesn't conflict with your values. You don't want to enhance that gap between perception, expectation and reality.

And in business don't forget to keep employees informed and updated, otherwise rumour and misinformation will fly around the organization.

A crisis needn't damage your reputation. When properly managed, it can provide an effective opportunity for communicating and demonstrating your values and integrity.

Examples of late payment letters

The Graphics Centre, Rowers' Green, Thameside T.. ...

Mr Sydney Beasley
The Corporation
Princes Way
Lower Town SE. ...

14 July 20—

Dear Mr Beasley,

Our Invoice No: 2389, 31 May 20— for £7,424

I am sorry to have to bring this to your attention, but the invoices for the work we undertook on your new brochure have yet to be paid and are now outstanding. As a very small concern, we operate on strict terms of 30 days. When payment was not received on the due date, 30th June, we submitted a reminder statement to your accounts department asking for payment by return, but two weeks onwards we have still not received any payment. We have telephoned twice but receive very unclear assurances about when payment may be expected.

As you know, we were delighted to accept this project, and undertook it in record time in order to meet your deadlines. We also have had expenses – the photographer and the artwork finisher – and, aware that they too as small businesses require payment on time, have already settled their accounts.

May we ask you to encourage your accounts department to settle our invoices within the next few days? We have always enjoyed working for your company and it would be a shame to let a matter such as this overshadow such a good relationship.

Yours sincerely,

Adrian Bellway

The Cleaning Company, 81 Ridgeway, Canterbury C.. ...

Mr Coates
The Accounts Department
Kent Cleaning Products
Canterbury KT.. ...

7 October 20 —

Dear Mr Coates,

Customer Reference No: 877904
Invoices 9306, 9307 & 9814

We have three invoices outstanding to your company, due for settlement at the end of October. The total sum is £5,100. Unfortunately The Cleaning Company has just lost one of its major clients. This is because the client has been taken over by another organization and at the moment they are unable to renew any suppliers' contracts. As it happens, ours was just due for renewal.

We are seeking reinstatement under the new regime and are actively seeking new work as well. However, this situation has left us very vulnerable financially in the short term. Would it be possible to arrange an extension of the payment period for these three invoices? We enclose a cheque for £1,000, and would ask if we could arrange to pay the balance by instalments: a further £500 at the end of October, £1,000 at the end of November, and £2,500 at the close of the year. We usually have a boost of work over the Christmas period and feel confident that we can clear the amount fully by then.

I am very sorry to have to ask you to help us in this way. We have had a very good relationship with your company for many years, and prefer your products to any others. This is the first time we have found ourselves in such circumstances, and we wish to assure you that we have every intention of honouring our debt. We just need a little time.

Yours sincerely,

Ralph Aykroyd

Chapter summary

- Agreements prevent misunderstandings
- Date your letter and specify all tasks and arrangements in detail and give any relevant timescales
- Use code numbers, references and full descriptions for any goods supplied or in a quotation
- Always write a dated covering letter for any documents sent by post or fax
- Confirm clearly arrangements and timings for payment

6
Invitations

6.1 IT'S A 'DO'!

It's a wedding, a party, a celebration, and you would like people to join you to make it a special and memorable occasion. You have the date, the time and the place, and now all you have to do is invite your guests.

There is usually a set form of words for very formal events – and for the subsequent replies – and there's an accepted form for less formal but still important rites of passage. For a casual 'do' you can have fun and be creative. Whatever the nature of the event, the basics are much the same. Your guests will need to know:

- the name of the host(s)
- the kind of event
- the date
- the time
- the venue
- the address to which replies should be sent (postal or even email)
- an indication of dress code, if appropriate

It is wise to send any invitation out in plenty of time to ensure that the maximum number of people will be available to come. For more informal parties, a few weeks may be sufficient; for a very formal wedding, one to two months may be better. Recently, 'Save the Day' cards have become fashionable. These are cards which announce the wedding (or major party) day, asking you to reserve the date in your diary, adding that formal invitations with full event details will come later.

6.2 THE WEDDING

We tend to revert to old-fashioned formulas and formality for life's major events, the most common being The Wedding. Even so, there are more variations simply because nowadays so many families experience divorce and remarriage, and there are many more multi-cultural marriages too. For weddings, unless it is to be a very small and private occasion, most people still prefer a formal printed invitation card, usually a folded 'book-shape'.

For most Christian and Jewish weddings, the usual format for printed invitations is:

Mr and Mrs Joseph Leadbetter
request the pleasure of your company
at the marriage of their daughter
Elspeth
to
Mr Harry Fox
at St Mawgan Parish Church, Newquay
on Saturday, 7th May, 20—
at 2.30 p.m.
and afterwards at
the Bedruthan Steps Hotel, Mawgan Porth

RSVP
   4 Europa Crescent
     Mawgan Porth
      Cornwall

RSVP is after the French, *répondez s'il vous plaît*, literally meaning, reply, if you please. The address you show after the RSVP is not necessarily that of the hosts, but where you wish the replies to go. See Chapter 7 p. 115 for the accepted form of how to respond to formal invitations such as these.

If the mother and father of the bride are divorced and – in this case – Mrs Leadbetter has not remarried, the first line can read: *Mr Joseph Leadbetter and Mrs Jane Leadbetter*. If Mrs Leadbetter has remarried and become Mrs James Brown, the first line can read: *Mr Joseph Leadbetter and Mrs James Brown*.

If Mrs James Brown is hosting the wedding with her new husband, the first lines would read: *Mr and Mrs*

James Brown request the pleasure of your company for the marriage of her daughter, Elspeth.

Nowadays there is an increasing number of marriages between divorced people and older people, where parents are no longer alive. In this instance, the wedding invitation may be:

> *Miss Elspeth Leadbetter and Mr Harry Fox*
> *request the pleasure of your company*
> *at their marriage*

or, in the case of divorcees, who may be having a civil ceremony, followed by a church blessing:

> *Mrs Jane Leadbetter and Mr James Brown*
> *request the pleasure of your company*
> *at a blessing of their marriage*

In all these instances, you will wish to ensure that the recipients know who in their family or group is included in the invitation. One way is to write the names in the top right-hand corner. An alternative is to have the guests' names handwritten in the body of the invitation. In this case, the second line would read *request the pleasure of the company of,* followed by a space for the guests' names. If budget allows on this kind of bespoke invitation, you may wish to commission a calligrapher to write in the names.

If you do this pleasant task yourself, the names should always be written in ink, not ballpoint. Try using a calligraphy pen, or at the very least, one with an italic nib to add style to your writing. The usual greeting for children under fifteen is by forename only, so the guest line might read:

Mr and Mrs Joseph Leadbetter
request the pleasure of the company of
Mr and Mrs Wyatt, Richard and Simon [handwritten line]
at the marriage of their daughter
Elspeth
etc.

The time-honoured format for formal printed invitations is black copperplate script on one side only of a white, ivory or cream card. Decoration is usually simple, perhaps with a 'deckle' edging or a fine gold edging or bevel edge.

Usually the card will be either stand alone, i.e. a postcard, or 'fly', which is a card with a fold on the left, which stands upright like a book. Smythson of Bond Street say that card weights have increased over the years, and the smartest invitations are up to 600 grams in weight. People often request menu cards and place cards for the wedding reception to be in a matching style.

Most other faiths have invitations on much the same lines. One particularly charming addition is seen on Parsee wedding invitations. The last lines will often be the blessings of grandparents who have died and the compliments of aunts, brothers and sisters. For example:

Yasmin & Farokh Shavaksha Todywalla
cordially invite

....

to celebrate the wedding ceremony of their daughter
Marzbeen
with
Paurrushasp
(son of Sheru & Bomoshaw Cowasji Jila)
on Thursday, 4th April 2002, at 6.30 p.m.
Roz Sarosh Mah Ava, 1371, Y, Z.
at Jeejeebhoy Dadabhoy Agiary, Near Afghan Church,
Coloba, Mumbai 400 005 and to dinner thereafter

With the blessings of:	*With the compliments of:*
Late Jaloo & Shavaksha	*Dolly Nasserwanji Masalawalla*
* Rustomji Todywalla*	*Sam Munchersha Olpadwalla*
Late Nasserwanji Sorobji	*Pervin & Jeroo Shavaksha*
* Masalawalla*	* Todywalla*
	Kaizad & Malcolm Farokh
	* Todywalla*

[reproduced with the kind permission of Marzbeen and Paurrush Jila]

Interestingly, Marzbeen and her family also enclosed a small card, self addressed and stamped for replies, not only asking if invitees were able to come but checking whether they were vegetarian or non-vegetarian. We look at replies in the following chapter, but this seems an eminently sensible measure.

Titles: Titles, as well as military and police ranks, are used on formal invitations, including that of the groom. It would be wise to check the customs of the particular regiment or police service. (See also pages 12 to 18.)

Dress: It is considerate to let people know what's expected. If you want your guests to wear morning suits and top hats, specify that in a little handwritten note: *By the way, the majority of our gentleman guests will be wearing morning suits.* Most women wear hats to weddings but if the reception requires a change into evening dress, it is worth letting your guests know if and where there will be changing facilities. If the event requires black tie, i.e. dinner jackets (black or ivory jackets, and a bow tie), either include it on the invitation or in a separate note. *Decorations may be worn* is a good way of letting people know how formal the event is.

Some gentlemen's clubs require guests to wear jackets and ties. For example, the Royal Automobile Club in Pall Mall is among those that stick rigidly to this code, and their porters keep a couple of spare ties at the desk in case a guest is unaware of the stricture. The rules at the RAC are more relaxed at weekends but jeans are still not permitted in the dining areas, not even for breakfast. It's best to spell these expectations out to your guests so they are not embarrassed.

Nowadays, 'dress casual' means just that, and jeans may be expected.

6.3 LESS FORMAL WEDDINGS

Smaller, more private weddings do not necessarily require printed invitations, although thanks to computers, it is possible to print off small numbers. However, handwritten invitations – in ink rather than felt tip – are very acceptable. The wording may be very similar to the formal invitations or it can take the form of a letter:

> *103 Pendennis Lane*
> *Coventry CV. ...*
> *29th March, 20—*

Dear Andie,

Harry and I are to be married at St Mawgan Parish Church near Newquay on Saturday, 7th May at 12 noon. We are inviting only a small number of our closest friends to attend, and we both very much hope that you will be one of the party. Please do let us know if you are able to come. We will be having a wedding breakfast at the Bedruthan Steps Hotel, Mawgan Porth, afterwards.

> *With best wishes,*
> *Yours sincerely,*
>
> *Elspeth*

6.4 EXPERT ADVICE

Peter Lippiatt, Stationery Director at Smythson of Bond Street, stationers who are Royal Warrant holders, suggests:

Invitations can convey far more than practical details (host/hostess's name, whereabouts, time); they express a lot about the mood (informal/formal) of the event, dress codes and when guests are expected to leave. The best ones give plenty of information, so guests know whether or not to eat beforehand, arrange dinner afterwards or book babysitters. The expression 'till late' means no formal end time.

On all invitations, from the most formal to the most eccentric, these rules usually apply:

- Use heavy card (300–600 gms) as they may have to last for weeks or months.
- If engraving is too expensive, use flat, rather than thermographic, printing.
- Leave plenty of space around the words (large lettering can look corporate).
- Avoid rounded corners and very bright gold edging.
- Avoid unreadable typefaces, especially for postcodes.
- Because people have become so lax at replying, it is now common to put in a flat-printed reply card.

Traditionalists would avoid the words 'fork supper', 'lounge suit', 'invite' and 'dinner jackets'. For the latter, 'black tie' is better.

Formal Invitations – Key Phrases

The nature of your invitation will help people decide how formal or casual your event is. Usually, the more elegant your card, the grander the occasion. The use of the following phrases should let your guests know what to expect, and what is expected of them:

White Tie	Tail suits, with white bow tie, and usually a silk or embroidered waistcoat, for very grand evening events.
Morning Suit	Tailed suits, usually with a black jacket and grey striped trousers or a matching dark grey jacket and trousers, with a silk tie and a top hat. This attire is normally only for weddings and certain race meetings attended by royalty.
Black Tie	Black (or ivory) dinner jackets with a black bow tie and often a cummerbund. Men sometimes wear a coloured bow tie if the event is not too formal. For evening events only.
Informal	Lounge suits and a coloured tie.
Casual	Depends on the event: waxed jackets and wellingtons for winter country events, tee shirts and jeans for a barbecue, whatever

suits your 'set' for supper at a friend's home.

7.30 for 8 p.m.	Arrive between the two times. Usually drinks are served from 7.30 p.m. If it's a dinner it is possible that people will start to sit down at their tables at 8 p.m. with the first course served shortly afterwards. If it is a lecture, the organizers are hoping that the lecturer will be able to start promptly at 8 p.m.
Carriages at Midnight	People are expected to leave at midnight.
Cocktails	Usually from 6.30 to 8.30 p.m. Exotic drinks but often only nuts and crisps to eat.
Drinks and Canapés	Usually from 6.30 to 8.30 p.m. You are expecting people to go on to dinner.
Buffet	A fuller meal but eaten standing up.
Dinner Party	A formal dinner with a first course (or starter), main course, pudding and cheese.
Supper Party	A more informal meal, where starters are optional.

6.5 THE FORMAL PARTY

Bar Mitzvahs, 18th and 21st, 50th and 100th birthday parties, Silver, Golden and Diamond wedding anniversaries are all major celebrations and often the very best kind of excuse for a large party of family and friends. If the party is to be a formal affair, a printed invitation may be the best option. However, where special arrangements are being made – for car parking, for example – a separate note to those accepting may be very welcome. If people are travelling for some distance, it may also be valuable to have a simple map available. If the event is at a hotel or catering establishment, the venue may be able to provide you with a tried and tested map for guests.

Rabbi and Mrs Lionel Levington
request the pleasure of the company of

....

at a party
to celebrate the Bar Mitzvah of their son
Max
at The Mansion House Hotel, Liverpool
on Tuesday, 8th June, 20 —
at 7.30 p.m.

RSVP:
18 Ridgeway,
Liverpool

Mr and Mrs Mansel Arthur
request the pleasure of the company of
Mr & Mrs Norman Drysdale [handwritten line]
at a party
to celebrate their golden wedding anniversary
at The Headland Hotel, Swansea SW. ...
on Saturday, 17th June, 20—
at 8 p.m.

Black tie

RSVP
Wayside
The Village

Mrs Janet Mead
requests the pleasure of your company
at a dance
to celebrate the 18th birthday of her daughter
Betty
at the Ballroom
Meriden Hotel, Warwickshire
on Saturday, 29th July, 20—
at 7.30 p.m.

RSVP   *Carriages at 12 midnight*
Green Lane House
Stoneleigh, Warwickshire

The Chairman and Committee of the Greater London Group
of the Chartered Institute of Public Relations
request the pleasure of the company of
Cherry Chappell MCIPR
at the Savoy Hotel, London (River Room entrance, Savoy Place)
on Wednesday 17 November 2004
for champagne and dinner to mark the
21st anniversary of the founding of the GLG
decorations may be worn
champagne reception: 7 p.m. dinner: 7.30 p.m. dress: black tie

[reproduced by kind permission of the Greater London Group
of the Chartered Institute of Public Relations]

6.6 LESS FORMAL PARTIES

This is the opportunity for you to give your imagination full rein. Be sure that all the basic information is included: what it is, where it is, what date, at what time and to whom to reply. Otherwise, away you go!

Jill Lee is a picture framer who runs a print and framing shop in Fulham in south-west London. Her birthday invitations are now legendary amongst her friends. It started in the early 1980s with a handmade cocktail party invitation and grew from there.

Jill says: 'I like to echo the theme of the party, to give people a taste of what's to come. It gets people in the mood before they arrive. I usually make a tentcard, so it stands up on a shelf or dressing table, and I try to give people a surprise when they open it.'

In 1995, the year the National Lottery was started, Jill had the theme 'It could be you!' and gave everyone who came a lottery ticket. 'It's very difficult to get people to reply but on this occasion they had to RSVP in order to claim their ticket. It proved a real incentive but sadly no one won the million pounds.' There were other notable years:

- Each invitation boasted a tiny birthday cake candle with the invitation 'Come and Burn the Candle at Both Ends'.
- A strip cartoon from a national newspaper in which Jill added her own words to the speech bubbles.
- A fake fur fabric bear-like face, complete with studded eyes appliquéd to the card with the legend 'For a wild party, you party animal'. One of the guests turned his invitation into a mask and wore it that evening.
- A 'doctored' dollar bill.

Jill also suggests sending maps when the party is not at your home. You could even design invitation cards with the details of the date, time and venue running around the perimeter of a map of the area, ensuring that all your guests can find the event.

Another idea came from Gillian Swift, who has family connections with one of the major china manufacturers in Stoke-on-Trent. She chose to have a limited edition of a special plate made for her wedding invitations. The lettering was set out in black and gold on white bone china plates and the edges of the plates were perforated, rather like a doily, to allow for pretty ribbon to be threaded through and tied in a bow. They were much treasured by the recipients.

Chapter summary

- There are set styles for very formal events but casual invitations can be fun and creative
- Send invitations in plenty of time. Consider a 'Save the Day' card if you don't have all the details
- Most wedding and grand party invitations are printed on stiff card. Names of invitees can be handwritten
- Give the dress code either on the invitation or via a separate note
- If appropriate, send a map and details of where to park

7

Replies, Thanks and Congratulations

7.1 WHATEVER HAPPENED TO GOOD MANNERS?

Everyone moans about the dearth of good manners these days. Certainly what constitutes politeness has changed dramatically in the last decade, and some of the old ways appear outdated. However, I believe that kindness and thoughtfulness are still there, it's the style and pace at which we now live that are so different. But two of the many areas where we need a resurgence of old-fashioned courtesy are when someone has invited you to an event, large or small, and is extending hospitality to you, and when someone has given you a present, a good time or much needed help. We need to reply – and we should *always* say thank you.

In recent years, people have become very lax about replying promptly – or even at all – to invitations. One professional events organizer says that it's quite common, even when the event is highly desirable, to receive unprompted responses from less than half the people invited. Oddly enough, when they are prompted, some people are astonished you should ask them, because *of course* they are coming. How are you meant to know? Others pretend not to have seen the invitation. Then there are those who finally refuse, but only when really pushed to make a decision. This is so thoughtless to your hosts. What is unforgivable, unless some dire emergency has arisen, is to refuse the day before, or on the day of the event itself.

The tardy reply plays havoc with the numbers for catering – and anyway it is sloppy to the point of rudeness not to let your hosts know if you are attending. It doesn't take long to pen a postcard or note, or for the more informal approach to send an email, and your hosts will be reassured and pleased if you are looking forward to the 'do' that they are so carefully planning.

REPLIES

7.2 THE FORMAL REPLY

The response to a formal, third-person invitation is also in the third person. For example, you may receive an invitation that reads:

Mr & Mrs Smart
request the pleasure of
Miss Miti Ampoma
at a celebration of their Silver Wedding Anniversary
at the Grand Hotel, Lakeside
on 26th May, 20—
at 7 p.m.

RSVP: Jenny Smart
7 Belside
The Common, SW. ...

The response would therefore be:

> *Miss Miti Ampoma thanks Mr & Mrs Smart for their very*
> *kind invitation to celebrate their Silver Wedding Anniversary*
> *at the Grand Hotel, Lakeside on 26th May*
> *and is delighted to accept.*

The last line might also read *has much pleasure in accepting*.

or

> *Miss Miti Ampoma thanks Mr & Mrs Smart*
> *for their very kind invitation to celebrate their*
> *Silver Wedding Anniversary at the Grand Hotel, Lakeside*
> *on 26th May but regrets she is unable to attend.*

Another variation of the latter is:

> *Miss Miti Ampoma thanks Mr & Mrs Smart*
> *for their very kind invitation to celebrate their*
> *Silver Wedding Anniversary at the Grand Hotel, Lakeside*
> *on 26th May but, due to a previous*
> *engagement, she regrets she is unable to accept.*

If you are part of a couple or a family that receives an invitation, the same format of third person applies. You would then write: *Mr and Mrs Harry Gray thank Mr and Mrs Smart for their kind invitation ...* or *Mr and Mrs Harry Gray, Alison and Richard thank Mr and Mrs Smart . . .*

This may be correct but it is also very impersonal. If Miti, for instance, knows Mr and Mrs Smart very well, it is almost a put-down not to explain further. A way around this would be to make the usual formal 'regrets' and then add a covering note which explains the refusal in more personal terms. Miti might therefore add a short letter saying:

> *The House*
> *The Grove*
> *London W. ...*
> *22 June 20—*

Dear Bill and Jenny,

I am so very sorry that I won't be a part of your special celebration. By sad coincidence, this is also [the date of my sister's wedding/my partner's book launch/in the midst of my holiday to Tunisia]. What a shame! I am very disappointed.

I shall be in touch again on my return and I look forward to hearing all about it, seeing the photos, and hearing all the gossip.

My love and best wishes for a wonderful anniversary,
> *Miti*

7.3 LESS FORMAL REPLIES

These can be by a short letter, a note, a correspondence card or an email. The important thing is not only to send them, but to do so promptly. Nowadays, there is a huge array of correspondence cards to choose from.

Some people like to have their addresses and contact details printed on them, others prefer an art postcard or one with a favourite motif. The grander, personalized correspondence cards require matching envelopes, others need only the reply name and address written on the back, and the stamp.

THANK-YOUS

Thank-yous are important. They honour the giver and show that you haven't taken their generosity for granted, that you are pleased and you care about them. In some circumstances, thank-you letters may become things that are treasured. Whether the thank-you is for a present, a dinner or a holiday, or for helping you out, it should be a very personal communication, rather than in a format-style, and preferably handwritten.

Some stationers sell thank-you forms for wedding presents and even for presents for Christmas, birthdays and anniversaries. You simply fill in on a dotted line what the present was and sign the bottom. Donors' reactions to receiving one of these will differ, but I consider them merely a sort of acknowledgement or receipt, too impersonal to have any real meaning. If someone has taken the time and effort to select a special present, pay for it, wrap it in pretty paper and either mail or deliver it, the least the recipient can do is scribble a personal note.

If you are likely to receive a lot of presents – for a wedding, a special birthday or anniversary – it is a good idea to keep a list of what has arrived from whom. Sometimes, people bring their presents to the wedding reception or anniversary party. Quietly keeping a list may prove a valuable aide-memoire when you sit down later to write those thank-yous. Usually, the wedding and wedding anniversary letters are shared between the couple.

The same courtesy applies to birthday and Christmas presents. Someone has gone to the trouble of finding a present you might like. Children in my sphere know that it is wise to send me a thank-you, even if it is only an email. I have made it clear that, if I don't receive a thank-you, I will presume that they didn't like my present, and would therefore find presents from me unwelcome in the future. Sometimes the system crashes – the occasional lapse of manners is of course overlooked – but usually it does work. Peter Lippiatt at Smythson calls this system of encouragement 'two misses and you're out'.

Parents usually write on behalf of very small children. They should encourage slightly older children to write on their own. The letters or notes do not have to be examples of perfect grammar and punctuation. In fact, they can and should be fun and creative. One little chum emailed me a photograph of herself wearing the dressing gown I had just sent her for her birthday, holding a little banner with 'THANK YOU' written on it. Another, from Vienna, found writing in English a bit of a challenge so drew me pictures of her birthday cake and party. Who would not be charmed by that?

Thank-you letters do not have to be long. In fact, by and large, they sound more sincere if they are short and to the point. However, each one should contain something personal to the recipient. It's now perfectly acceptable to send a correspondence card, rather than a letter. If you send a picture postcard, it shows charm and consideration if the subject matter is appropriate either to the gift, the occasion or the recipient. I receive a lot of cards showing illustrations of cherries, in baskets, in bowls, on branches or simply as a motif. I am touched when anyone has bothered to find them.

Letters between friends thanking them for hospitality may be longer, of course, and so should letters thanking people for help given.

7.4 EXPERT ADVICE

Carole Stone, London's 'Queen of networking', is a self-confessed people addict. Her electronic contacts book bulges with over 25,000 people, many of them well known and prominent in their fields, as well as family and friends. She holds regular 'salons', bringing together friends and friends of friends, and a gigantic Christmas party, and her diary is full of business and social engagements. Says Carole:

Good manners are essential between friends, as they are in any relationship. The fact is that there are no shortcuts if you want to reap the real rewards of friendship. It's like everything else we do in life: don't skimp. If you do, your friendship will break down – just as the central heating does (when you really need some warmth badly) because you've not bothered to have the boiler regularly serviced. Friendships have to be looked after – nurtured – to make sure they're in good working order; they need to be taken care of. That care, I find, usually comes back to you later, in abundance.

Replying as early as possible to any kind of invitation is not just a courtesy – it's important. Whether a catering company is involved or a home-cooked supper round the kitchen table is the order of the day it's vital to know how many will be coming. And if it's a sit-down affair the host will want to know *who* is coming, so that they can be seated with people they will enjoy talking to. A 'maybe' is not a very helpful reply, unless you are already awaiting confirmation of another event that clashes with the date – in which case it is better to make personal contact by phone to explain the position.

Don't be someone who says yes to every invitation and then cancels when a better offer comes along – this is the sure way to lose friends. Of course there is always the possibility of something essential cropping up that means you have to pull out – but again this should be done in a personal phone call – certainly not via a secretary! If it's a business event you've been invited to then it may be helpful if you can suggest someone else who might replace you.

Thank-you notes are something your host will always be pleased to receive – I positively treasure them! Try to send a handwritten letter rather than an email, certainly for a lunch, dinner or a party – anything more than just a drink. Include something about the occasion you particularly enjoyed – that amazing pudding, that stimulating conversation about American politics – or a line that says 'it was a bonus to meet your charming children Tom and Jo'. Mention one or two people you enjoyed talking to – 'what a pleasure to see Linda Cooper again' – or remark on something you liked about your host's home.

Thank-you notes should always be sent when someone has done you a good turn, though in this case an email might be enough: 'thank you so much for putting me in touch with your gardener, he is coming to see me next Monday', or 'thank you for telling Mary that I was looking for a new job'. And don't forget to tell people who gave you an idea for something what became of it. People want to know what happened to their suggestion, and that's how friendships grow.

Examples of thank-yous
For the wedding/anniversary present

Tall Trees
The Grove
Forest of Dean

4th May 20—

Dear Mr and Mrs Black,

Ian joins me in thanking you for the beautiful cream towels you sent us as a wedding present. These will look gorgeous in our newly painted bathroom, which is cream and silver.

We were so sorry that you were unable to come to the wedding, although we quite understand that your holiday was booked long before we knew our date. Did you have a good time? What we are hoping is that you will come soon and tell us all about it, and we will try not to be too boring about our wedding party!

Again, our thanks for the lovely thick towels.

With very best wishes,

Jane and Ian

Tall Trees
The Grove
Forest of Dean

4th May 20—

Dear Greg and Amanda,

Wherever did you find it! You are geniuses. Jane joins me in sending you huge thanks for the fantastic retro radio which is by far one of our favourite wedding presents. It sits in Fifties splendour on the shelves in the sitting room and we smile every time we play it, which is daily.

It was great to see you at the wedding. We are biased of course but we thought it was a fun do. Please come and see us soon.

Until then, know that you made two newly weds very happy.

All the best,

Ian and Jane

For the birthday present (child)
[card]

Dear Uncle Jack and Aunty Christi,

Thank you very much for the £5 you sent me for my birthday. It was a nice surprise when it fell out of my card! I will be taking it to spend on my holiday. We are going to Scotland in a few weeks.

Lots of love,

Luca

For having me/us to stay

London SW. ...

20 June 2005

Dear Thomas and Marina,

I cannot thank you enough for such a wonderful stay. I enjoyed it all so much. The day trip to the Wachau was particularly special, and Nigl was a fabulous restaurant. Great choice, Thomas! And, of course, Don Carlos at the Opera House was magical.

Treats though they were, most of all, I enjoyed the dinner parties with the family. The children are growing up so quickly and they are such fun.

I cannot begin to return your hospitality but I will ensure that you are well wined and dined when you next come to London.

With love and best wishes,

Cherry [signed]

For the dinner/party
[card]

Dear Jackson and Evette,

What a fabulous dinner party! Clever you, it was a great combination of people; they were all interesting and outgoing and mixed well, and the food was a triumph. I would particularly like the recipes for the couscous dish and, on Liam's request, that lethal creamy lemon pudding. Thank you both for inviting us: we had a terrific time.

Love from
Ellie and Liam

For a child's birthday party
[card]

Dear Mrs West,

Thank you so much for inviting Sam to Alex's birthday party last Saturday. He had the most marvellous time and couldn't stop talking about it afterwards. He was also thrilled that he won a prize in one of the games.

I expect we will see one another again soon at the school but in the meantime, many thanks again for having Sam.

All good wishes,

Jennie Brown

For helping out (neighbour/friend)

52 Pepworth Drive
Hastings H.. ...
8 November 20 —

Dear Edna,

I cannot tell you how grateful I have been for all your help over the last few months and I want to put it on record. I had no idea how vulnerable breaking an ankle can make you! But, of course, it was not just me who was affected but dear little Clemmie. I felt that it was almost too much that you should walk her every day, but coming as you did twice daily meant that she was exercised as normal and hardly noticed the difference!

It was also a joy to have you calling in, and I shall miss that. However, as you know, I am becoming very mobile again and the exercise is good for me as well as Clemmie.

You hold a very special place in our hearts, and I hope that you will continue to pop in for tea as often as you like. Thank you, thank you for all your kindness.

With fondest wishes,

James

For volunteering

Dear Rosie,

Just a note to thank you for all your time and hard work in making the Flower Festival such a success. I don't know how we would manage without you, and it tickles us to bits to see you round up all your family and friends to help run the cream teas.

Once again, as you know, we had a record number of visitors and we raised well over £3,000 for the church. It was a terrific effort, and it can only happen when there is such an efficient and dedicated team behind it.

By the way, we thought your set piece, Angels in a Garden, was hugely creative and attractive.

Again, thank you for a magnificent contribution!

Best wishes,

Andrew Aintree

For sponsoring me

> *— Alma Road*
> *Plymouth PL.. 4..*
> *20 May 20—*

Mr M. Turner
Director & General Manager
Pall Newquay
St Columb
Cornwall TR9 6TT

Dear Mr Turner,

Thank you so much for your generous donation towards my fundraising on behalf of the Chestnut Appeal. Your contribution of £100 was very much appreciated.

Yours sincerely,

Chris Herbertson

[reproduced by kind permission of Christine Herbertson who took part in a trek to Namibia to raise funds for a dedicated unit for the treatment of prostate cancer at Derriford Hospital in Plymouth. Overall she raised £1,800]

CONGRATULATIONS

Life has so many downsides and quandaries, it's always wonderful to hear – and share in – any good news. When someone has achieved something, gained a promotion or an award, or won a race, a prize or one of life's other trophies, it adds to their pleasure and confirms your friendship, if you send a note of congratulations. There's nothing like receiving praise from people we care about. It boosts us, give us confidence, and probably even strengthens our immune systems.

Examples of letters of congratulation

Chelsea, London
June 2005

Dear Florian,

I've just heard from your father that you have passed all your exams this term, and many of them with distinction. Well done! I know that you must have worked extra hard after the struggles of last year. This is indeed a triumph and you can be extremely proud of yourself. Now you can enjoy the rest of summer!

Love from
Cherry

Wayside
St Nicholas
Cardiff

3rd January, 20—

Dear Dr West,

My wife and I have just heard that you have received an OBE in the New Year's Honours list, and we would like to offer you our sincere congratulations. Your work for the hospital trust, the regional health authority and the medical community alone would warrant such an honour, but you also do so much for charity in the area. I particularly remember how much support you gave to us when we were raising funds for the church.

We are delighted that your contribution has been properly acknowledged in this way and we hope that you enjoy the ceremony at Buckingham Palace. We look forward to seeing the photos in the local paper!

Yours sincerely,

Adrian and Grace Bestow

Chapter summary

- Never forget to reply, preferably early – it flatters your hosts and helps decide the catering numbers
- There is a set style for formal invitations but you can always add a personal note
- Thank-you letters do not have to be long – but, like all good manners, are always appreciated
- If someone you know has done well, congratulate them

8

Condolence and Illness

8.1 THE DIFFICULT LETTERS

There are certain kinds of letter which most people, even those who are fluent letter writers in normal circumstances, find particularly difficult to write. These are letters of sympathy, related to illness and to death. There are three sets of circumstances which call for such letters.

First of all, many of us face the sad task of writing to someone who has become seriously ill or severely injured, when an overly jolly greetings card might strike a strident note. To send a 'Get Well' card to someone who you know is facing terminal illness, or the prospect of permanent disability, would be deeply unfeeling. Hard though it may be to find the right words, it might be much kinder to send a little handwritten note of support. That's not to suggest that humour and levity would be inappropriate. In fact, they can be enormously appreciated and even strengthening.

Secondly, at some stage in our lives most of us have

to announce the death of someone we love, and inform family and friends of the subsequent funeral arrangements. These are necessities at a poignant time, and some people find that it is easier to write than to phone and hear the grief of others. There are also the official letters and notices and it sometimes seems incongruous to write so dispassionately about something so emotionally charged.

Finally, we may also have the occasion to write a letter of condolence. This is possibly the most taxing of all to put together, particularly when we have cared for the person who has died. While aware of how much consolation such letters can give to the bereaved, there is always the worry that the letter might bring extra tears or in some way be insensitive.

In all three of these instances, it should be remembered that messages in letters and cards are tributes and therefore of enormous importance to the recipients. They are tangible examples of the affection, appreciation and high regard in which someone is or was held. No matter how difficult or painful the act of writing them may be, these letters can be of immense, lasting value and comfort.

WHEN SOMEONE IS ILL

When you hear that someone you know has a long-term illness, or one where there is little hope of recovery, or a severe disability or injury, put yourself in their shoes just for a moment. They may still be in their own home, or in a hospital, nursing home or hospice. Wherever they are, they still have life to live, even if it has become a matter of quality, rather than quantity. No matter how debilitating their condition, they will still want to be a part of life and to know that they are valued.

Nothing could be more likely to contribute to their decline than when people, through a kind of strange embarrassment, ignore them, or fail to honour their fight for dignity and a measure of independence, or isolate them from the parts of life to which they might still contribute.

Letters should certainly be sympathetic and support-ive but they can also be upbeat. The underlying mes-sages – however you choose to express them – are most probably that:

- We care about you.
- We are sorry this has happened to you.
- We want you to be strong.
- We are there for you when you don't feel so brave.
- Otherwise, as far as we are concerned, it is business as usual for as long as it's possible.

As a friend with an aggressive terminal condition once said to me, 'I can't sit around for months just dying, and I certainly don't want to be treated as though I am dying. I really want to enjoy as much as possible of what's left. I want to see the people I care about, drink wine, dance when I'm able, and hear the birds sing.' And so he did.

It is all depends on the personality of the person you are writing to, but the chances are that they will like to hear about positive or funny things as well as being reassured that you haven't forgotten them.

Ensure that you write in the present tense. It's very easy, when you know someone will not recover, to start using the past tense. They are still alive and may feel you are being premature. Use phases like *You are always such a tower of strength of us* rather than *You have always been such a tower of strength*.

8.2 EXPERT ADVICE

Nick Gundry, a counselling pyschologist from Budock in Cornwall, says:

It's important not to become bogged down with words and language, or adopt a different persona, because the situation is serious or even tragic. Just be yourself. Your relationship with someone who has become ill or who is bereaved is the same as it always was, so suddenly to become more formal or flowery is artificial. Say things in the way you would normally.

Try to avoid philosophizing on the meaning of life and certainly don't be tempted to say that you know how someone feels, however close a friend or relative they are. Avoid relating what has happened in similar circumstances and never point out it's 'just like when Uncle George died'. To the bereaved person, what they are experiencing is wholly personal, unique. Brevity is fine; don't feel you have to offer advice or give a parable!

When someone is under stress, they hang on to what is positive and familiar, so acknowledge their loss – of their health or of a person – but then communicate in a way that is appropriate to the person receiving it.

Examples of letters of sympathy

The Firs,
Wrights Lane,
Warston, W.. ...
4 February 20—

Dear Richard,

John and I were so very sorry to learn about your accident. What a dreadful thing. I contacted [your brother/mother/partner] right away for an update and [he/she] tells me that you may experience some long-term problems as a result, and that is the hardest part of all.

It's no surprise to hear that you are tackling your treatment and recovery with enormous courage. You are always such a brave heart. We're immensely proud of you. As soon as you are up to visitors, be prepared for us to traipse in.

In the meantime, we are holding you in our thoughts and prayers.

Yours sincerely,

Wendy and John

29 Boltons Lane
Hardcastle
H.. ...

30 April 20—

Dear Aunt Mavis,

I am extremely sorry to hear that there's been a recurrence of the cancer. It seems so unfair to have this setback when you have already been through so much. Brave lady that you are, you deserve the very best life can offer.

I appreciate that you will be undergoing further treatment and you will need to concentrate your energies. If you would like some company, we will be delighted to come for an hour or an afternoon – we'll be guided by you. In fact, when you are up for it, I could do with a gossip. You always give me such wonderfully sensible advice and I would welcome your thoughts on an opportunity that has arisen for me at work. I am very happy to come to you.

Incidentally, Sophie joins Deon and me in sending our love and best wishes. She is dizzy with delight at the moment because her exam results were even better than she expected. She now has four GCSEs.

We all want to tell you that we're here for you, any time of the night or day.

Love from

Andrew, Deon – and Sophie!

[to the partner of a colleague]

Melrose Ltd, Sydney Lane, London SW. ...

18 June 20—

Dear Alan,

I have heard via the company that your wife is very ill and I am writing to tell you how very sorry I am.

This is a very difficult time for you too: you must be so worried. Please let me know if there is any practical way in which I can help. I would be only too pleased to take over some of the workload for the time being. There are others in the department who feel just the same. Just give me a call. In the meantime, all your colleagues here join me in sending our greatest sympathies.

Yours sincerely,

David
Accounts Department

The 21st Regiment Dining Club, Little Nettleton,
Gloucester GL.. ...
17 September 20—

Dear Mrs Monkton,

We are very sorry to hear that Tom is unwell. As you know, your husband has been a longstanding and well-liked member of this club for many years.

We understand that you are visiting him daily and wonder if all the driving is becoming a burden to you. If so, several of the members here would be pleased to arrange a rota of lifts. Please let me know if this would be of value to you.

We will be writing to Tom at the hospital, but we realize what a difficult time this is for you and send you our greatest sympathies.

Yours sincerely,
[signature]
Philip Anstey (Major)

ANNOUNCING THAT SOMEONE HAS DIED

There is really no easy way to soften the announcement. If you wish, you can use phrases such as 'passed away' or 'slipped away' but, nowadays, most people prefer to say 'died'. A notice in local newspapers can be one way of announcing the death and the details of the funeral to people in your area.

You can also arrange for cards to be printed and mailed to acquaintances, former colleagues and to clubs and associations. Even so, there will still be a number of closer relatives and friends who will expect a more personal form of communication.

8.3 NEWSPAPER NOTICE

Often funeral directors will help you to formulate the wording. They may even have an established arrangement with local newspapers for placing notices on your behalf. If you are organizing the notices yourself, you will find that many newspapers have a set format and the staff in the classified advertisements department are usually extremely helpful. Otherwise you may choose something on the lines of:

Helen Brown and Frank Smith
in great sadness announce the death
of their mother, Agnes Smith, on 23 November 20—
The funeral will be held at St Bride's, Alverston Avenue at 11 a.m.
on 30 November. No flowers: donations to Cancer Research UK

or

Smith, Agnes, on 23 November 20—, peacefully at St Saviour's Hospice, aged 85 years. Beloved widow of the late Geoffrey and much loved mother of Helen Brown and Frank Smith. Funeral service at St Bride's, Alverston Avenue, 30 November at 11 a.m. Family flowers only, donations in lieu if desired to Cancer Research UK

8.4 LETTERS

The initial letter can be very brief. Later, or to a special friend or relative, you may wish to write at some length, but in the early days, when there are so many arrangements to be made, a short note is perfectly acceptable.

Examples of death announcement letters

51 Marywood Avenue
Birmingham B.. ...

4 October 20—

Dear Uncle Rupert,

I know that you will be sorry, although not surprised, to hear that Mummy died yesterday morning. The hospice was wonderful and her last hours were without pain. I was at her side and can tell you that she left us peacefully.

The arrangements for the funeral are now underway and we anticipate that it will be on Tuesday next at St Bride's Church. I will confirm the actual times and practical details in a day or two.

With love and sympathy from
Annie

51 Marywood Avenue
Birmingham B.. ...

8 October 20—

Dear Mr Allen,

It is with great sadness that I must tell you of my mother's death last Monday. As you know, she had been ill for some months and she spent her last days at St Saviour's Hospice.

Her funeral will be at St Bride's Church, on Tuesday next, 11 October, at 11 a.m. We hope that, as such a longstanding and loyal friend of my mother's, you will be able to come. There will only be flowers from close family. Otherwise, we are asking everyone to make a donation in lieu of flowers to St Saviour's Hospice to help them continue their wonderful work.

There will be a short reception at my mother's home afterwards.

Yours sincerely,

Annie Blackburn

51 Marywood Avenue
Birmingham B.. ...

8 October 20—

Messrs Anstey & Co
Solicitors
161 High Road
Birmingham B.. ...

Dear Sirs,

I wish to inform you of the death of my mother, Mrs Rowena Jackson, on Monday, 3 October. Her death was registered the following day and I enclose a copy of her death certificate.

I see from her records that you hold her will. I am informing her executors of the situation and will be meeting them after the funeral on Tuesday next. I look forward to hearing from you about what is now necessary.

Yours faithfully,

Annie Blackburn

CONDOLENCE

It can be extremely isolating to be bereaved. Not only have bereaved people lost someone they cared about, but their friends and colleagues are suddenly unsure of how to treat them or what to say to them. As a result, some people choose not to say anything, and stay at a distance, even though they may be deeply sympathetic and caring, and may themselves be grieving on some level for the person who has died.

If you know someone who is bereaved, you may find that you are unable to express yourself in person, for whatever reason, but you may wish to write to demonstrate your sympathy and support.

Sometimes you will know both the bereaved and the person who has died; at other times you will know one party or the other. In the first instance you may have some idea of what might be of comfort to the bereaved person. It's important to acknowledge both what the person who has died has meant to you, and your feelings for – and support of – the person you are writing to.

If they were very close to the person who has died, the bereaved will be in shock during the early days, even if the death was expected. Later, they may be more accepting of the fact of the death, but nonetheless may be grieving every bit as much.

Frequently, part of the grieving process is linked to guilt; we feel guilty because we didn't do more, take the pain or the whole problem away. When you know such feelings are unjustified, you may wish to use reassuring phrases in your letter, such as *your father was always so proud of you* and *you were a marvellous son to him, and could not have done more to help him.* These kinds of comments may bring very real comfort.

Often, when we feel upset ourselves or are embarrassed by the emotional grief of others, we take the shortcut of using platitudes. In fact, platitudes are better than not writing at all, but there are ways of doing it better. This may involve us examining our personal feelings about what is valuable in our own as well as other people's lives. For instance, it is unlikely that we would want to write about someone's enormous wealth, but we may wish to acknowledge that they were entrepreneurial and built up a highly successful business, or had made a wonderful home where family and friends were always welcome. It is doubtful that you would share that someone had a big new car every year, but you may well pay homage to their support for charities or their service or commitment to their community.

Condolence is a way of paying tribute to those aspects of a person's life that the bereaved will wish to have acknowledged and confirmed by others. It is possible we know that the person who has died has not always acted well; this is the time to avoid brutal honesty, although it may be kinder to do so by omission rather than falsifying the truth. Even in grief, the bereaved will be able to spot insincerity. So, for example, if the person who has died was frequently bad tempered, concentrate instead on some quality that was more positive, perhaps their quick wit or their loyalty to their family and friends.

Remember to sympathize with the loss the bereaved will be feeling. While expressing your own feelings of grief, try to give some measure of comfort to those whose feelings will be even more acute.

At the same time it is worth bearing in mind that the bereaved sometimes keep the condolence letters to read again at some future time or even to pass on to future generations. Never write something that you will later regret.

8.5 EXPERT ADVICE

John Jackson-Okolo, a bereavement counsellor in London, says:

> We all have different experiences of bereavement and this can relate to differences in cultures, age, religious convictions, the circumstances of the death, and so on. It's important not to make assumptions about how others may feel. Counsellors always work from their clients' perspectives – putting themselves in their shoes – working towards empathy. It will depend on your relationship with the person you are writing to, of course, but it's worth making this your starting point.
>
> There is always a lot happening in the period immedi-

ately after someone has died, with the funeral and the arrangements about the effects, but it's six months down the line that people feel isolated. The grief process is still being worked through. Maybe this is a good time, if you haven't seen the person, to follow up on your initial letter.

Examples of condolence letters

29 Burnaby Grove
Manchester M. ...

5th May 20—

Dear Mary,

The whole family is distressed to hear about your mother's death. We had known her for more than thirty years, and she was much loved by us all.

I will remember her for many reasons. She was always very kind to me, as she was to so many others. She welcomed me into your home in good times and bad and, as you probably remember, I spent long hours sitting at her kitchen table resolving my life, with her offering much needed advice. She never failed to make time for people in trouble. That's a rare gift. So was her sense of the ridiculous, which was quite wicked at times!

We were all aware that she was ailing and of course we would not have wanted her to stay if there was pain and a poor quality of life. Even so, this is very hard on you. I know how close the two of you were and I can only begin to imagine how much you will miss her. Call on us at any time you wish, for practical things or just for the company of people who loved Joan and will never forget her.

With love and much sympathy,

Leah

42 Malvern Way
Stoke-on-Trent ST. ...

2nd December 20—

Dear Mr Green,

My wife Sybil and I were very saddened by the death of your father, Jacob. He lived next door to us for almost ten years and we were very fond of him. He was always such a courteous gentleman, with wonderful old-fashioned manners, and he never failed to smile and chat, even though we knew he was plagued by painful arthritis in recent years.

We haven't met but we feel we know you from your father's comments and stories. He was extremely proud of you and always thoroughly enjoyed his visits to your home at Christmas. Please accept our condolences at your loss.

Yours sincerely,

Jack Haines

21 Tredragon Lane
Taunton
Somerset TA. ...

8 May 20—

Dear Yvonne,

I have just heard through the church that your sister in Reading has died. How dreadfully sad for you. I don't think I ever met her, but I did meet your mother on one occasion and I know what a rare and happy family you were. Losing a sibling is terribly hard. We expect them to be with us throughout our lives.

I understand that you will be travelling up and down to Reading in the next few weeks. When you have more time, do phone or call round for coffee.

All sympathy,

Maia

Chapter summary

- These may be the hardest letters to write but they mean a great deal to the recipients
- These letters are tributes and should be positive and affectionate
- Don't philosophize or use special flowery language. Acknowledge the situation and the loss without embarrassment, and demonstrate your sympathy and support
- If you are announcing that someone has died, the initial letter can be brief. Later you may wish to write at greater length
- Try not to use platitudes, but even platitudes are better than not writing at all

9
Love and Friendship Letters

9.1 A LIFE IN LETTERS

Biographers of the future will face an immense challenge. Many biographies are entirely dependent on letters sent, received and carefully kept, not just for an accurate interpretation of the facts about someone's life, but for a sense of their reality, and their context in their personal and wider histories. Because of telephones and emails, 21st-century people don't write social letters in the way that our forebears did. As a consequence, we will have few records of people's feelings, beliefs and reactions in the way that we did in the past. It's a great pity.

If you read the letters that Wolfgang Amadeus Mozart sent regularly to his father in Salzburg, to his sister and friends, to his wife when they were apart, and to his various patrons and colleagues, you can begin to gain a sense of his exuberant personality, his humour and energy, and also of the turbulent times he lived in. His thoughts flowed on to paper in a stream of consciousness that permits us to hear his authentic

voice, understand his problems, frustrations and
enthusiasms – and appreciate his music even more. He
was in Budwitz (now in the Czech Republic), en route
to Berlin via Prague, Dresden and Leipzig, when he
scribbled this delightful message – which I believe perfectly reflects his temperament – to his wife, Constanze,
in Vienna:

8 April 1789

Dearest little Wife!

*While the prince is off bargaining for fresh horses, I am seizing
this opportunity with great pleasure to write to you, dearest little
wife of my heart, a few quick words. – How are you? – Are you
thinking of me as often as I am thinking of you? – I look at your
portrait every few minutes – and cry – half out of joy, half out
of sorrow! – Please look after your health, which is so dear to
me, and stay well, my darling! – And don't worry on my account,
because I am suffering no hardships on this trip – no adversities
– except your absence – which, as it can't be helped, simply must
be endured. – I am writing this with tears in my eyes; – adieu
– I'll write more from Prague – and I'll also write more legibly
because I won't have to be in such a rush – adieu – I kiss you
most tenderly a Million times and remain Forever your*

stu – stu* Mozart
faithful unto death

*meaning unknown

[From: *Mozart's Letters, Mozart's Life* – selected letters edited
and newly translated by Robert Spaethling, Faber and Faber,
2000]

In her book *A Profound Secret*, Josceline Dimbleby writes about the close relationship between her great-grandmother May Gaskell and the Pre-Raphaelite painter Sir Edward Burne-Jones. Although married to other people, they corresponded prolifically – up to five letters a day – for many years until Burne-Jones's death in 1898.

Two years after he had started this correspondence, Sir Edward Burne-Jones maintained that during that time he had sent her over seven hundred letters. It is interesting that at one stage he appears concerned that she might be overwhelmed by this attention, writing:

I am always, all day long, wanting to talk myself out to you – for with you only I think aloud – and that is easy and happy it has been a wonderful fortune for me to have known you – in a moment when I am with you all fatigue and wear of life and all sadness disappears, by nothing less than magic – and I am ten years old again . . . do you like me to write so much, or is it overmuch – pretend you like it for it makes my chief happiness – verily it does – goodbye – oh it is hard to leave and yet am I not always and every moment your E.

[From: *A Profound Secret* by Josceline Dimbleby, Doubleday 2004, Black Swan, 2005]

Josceline Dimbleby points out: 'Although the Victorians were more formal than we are in social conversation, they were far less inhibited about revealing their innermost feelings and emotions when they wrote letters. Few of us now, for fear of ridicule, dare expose our sentiments, even privately, in the way that our ancestors did. The Victorians and Edwardians expressed affection for their friends in a way that only lovers, and perhaps not many of them, would choose to do now.'

I believe that this is a shame. Perhaps we would not wish to express ourselves quite so floridly as the Victorians, but not to let your friends know that you care for and appreciate them can only diminish the relationship.

9.2 LETTERS TO FRIENDS AND FAMILY

We deal with replies, thank-yous and congratulations in Chapter 7, and letters of condolence and those in response to news of illness or disability in Chapter 8. For the more usual run of letters to distant friends and family, there are no rules beyond having fun. Edward Burne-Jones often illustrated his letters with sketches and cartoons. You can do the same. Be creative. You could include other tokens, if they might amuse or bring pleasure: photographs, of course, but also magazine or newspaper cuttings, recipes, pressed flowers, a wine or beer label, a menu, quotes from books or newspapers, or even locks of baby hair. You can write as you would talk to that person, or make the letter a kind of diary.

If you enjoy this kind of creative letter-writing, you might also consider finding a pen pal. There are people of all nationalities, ages and interests who also enjoy this kind of correspondence. If you look on the Internet there are all kinds of organizations which set up pen friends, ranging from associations of school children and religious groups to the purely social.

For many years, I have written to a relative in Australia. We both have email but, by and large, we prefer to send each other old-fashioned long gossipy letters every month or six weeks. We recount not only the major events of our lives, but also share the minutiae; I know a lot about the mulching of gardens in Toowoomba. I have never met this relative, although I hope to soon. And when I do, I trust that it will only enhance this very special relationship-by-letter.

9.3 LOVE LETTERS

In days gone by, love letters were treasured possessions, to be tied in pretty ribbon and kept safely. They were the only means of distant communication between close friends and lovers; there were no phones or email, just the post. Care was taken with the paper and ink, with special seals and initials or phrases with secret meanings.

Times of war and adversity seem to bring a fluency that isn't accessible in more peaceful times. Soldiers in the First World War – and conflicts before and since – went into the trenches carrying their wives' or sweethearts' letters in their pockets, reminders of love and home comforts, while they were at the gates of hell. Such spare time as they had was often spent in composing letters to send home. Sadly, sometimes these proved to be the final dispatches, received and treasured by grieving wives and girlfriends.

The Geneva Convention, relating to the treatment of prisoners of war, acknowledges the vital importance of letters. Article 71 states that 'Prisoners of war shall be allowed to send and receive letters and cards. If the Detaining Power deems it necessary to limit the number of letters and cards sent by each prisoner of war, the said number shall not be less than two letters and four cards monthly.' It was accepted, however, that a level of censorship would be likely.

Obviously people nowadays have exactly the same feelings for one another that they did in the past and still enjoy expressing them. A young barrister I know often emails love messages to her husband who works in the City. He isn't quite so fluent, but responds with flowers and bottles of her favourite perfume.

For once, there are few guidelines. Creativity is all, sincerity is the only criterion. Counselling psychologist Nick Gundry suggests: 'A love letter should be a true expression of the writer's emotion. Don't be trapped into trying to write a poetic epic unless of course you happen to be a talented poet. Otherwise, you could end up sounding false, corny, or even ridiculous. Just express what you feel.'

At the same time, a love letter is an opportunity to put down in detail what, at that given moment, you may feel you cannot say face-to-face. If you run dry of ideas, you can always borrow from the greats, although it may be wise to acknowledge the true authors, on the lines of 'as Napoleon wrote to his Josephine . . .'. It would be embarrassing later if someone spotted that the quotations were not your own.

Another idea is to look up the lyrics of your favourite songs. There are songs, old and new, which express every nuance, every variation of sentimental feeling, so maybe you can find one which says something about what you want to express. Think of the Leonard Cohen line from 'Chelsea Hotel No. 2' – *You told me again you preferred handsome men / but for me you would make an exception* or Neil Diamond and Barbra Streisand's 'You Don't Bring Me Flowers' – *So you think I could learn how to tell you goodbye / . . . because you don't say you need me.* You might wish to write in the language of love, and French still does it for some of us; consider Nina Simone's 'Ne Me Quitte Pas' (original lyrics by Jacques Brel) – *Moi, je t'offrirai des perles de pluie, venues de pays ou il ne pleut pas* (loosely: 'I'll give you pearls of rain from countries where it doesn't rain').

A friend of mine sighs even now over a man who would regularly sent her postcards bearing little snippets of lyrics. When their affair finished, she sent him one with a few lines from Pink Floyd's 'Wish You Were Here' –

We're just two lost souls, swimming in a fish bowl, year after year
Running over the same old ground. What have we found? The same old fears
Wish you were here.

(Waters, Gilmour)

You could take song lyrics and adapt them to suit you and your love. You might even add 'Sing to the tune of . . .'. Have fun; for instance you can make up your own secret codes. Sophie Lazar, my editor at Penguin, suggests writing so that the first and last word of every sentence when strung together give directions to a meeting place, or sending instructions on how to fold the notepaper so it will reveal a special message.

You can also scour the poetry books. Some of the new poets are fun and quirky – think of Wendy Cope – and there are always the 'classics' such as Elizabeth Barrett Browning's famous but always very moving Sonnets from the Portuguese.

If you look carefully at the examples we show here, you will find that you can identify certain recurring themes and may be able to find your own way to express them.

All the examples in this chapter have been chosen because they are very revealing in some way of the nature of the love affair. For example, in the extract from a much longer letter shown below, Napoleon Bonaparte shows a surprising level of self-awareness of his immense ambition, even admitting that it was undermining his relationship with the woman he loved so passionately. This was written in 1796, when he was on his Italian campaign, the year after he and Josephine had married:

To citizen Bonaparte
care of citizen Beauharnais
6, rue Chantereine
Paris

Nice, 10 Germinal, year IV

I have not spent a day without loving you; I have not spent a night without embracing you; I have not so much as drunk a single cup of tea without cursing the pride and ambition which force me to remain separated from the moving spirit of my life. In the midst of my duties, whether I am at the head of my army or inspecting the camps, my beloved Josephine stands alone in my heart, occupies my mind, fills my thoughts. If I am moving away from you with the speed of the Rhône torrent, it is only that I may see you again more quickly. If I rise to work in the middle of the night, it is because this may hasten by a matter of days the arrival of my sweet love . . .

. . . My heart, obsessed by you, is full of fears which prostrate me with misery . . . I am distressed not to be calling you by name, I shall wait for you to write it.

Farewell! Ah! if you love me less you can never have loved me. In that case I shall be truly pitiable.

Bonaparte

[From: *The Lover's Companion*, edited by Elizabeth Jane Howard, David and Charles, Newton Abbot]

Nomzamo Winifred (Winnie) Madikizela married Nelson Mandela in 1958, becoming his comrade in the fight against apartheid in South Africa. Nelson was imprisoned from 1963 onwards. The letter below written by Winnie in 1985, after more than twenty years of enforced separation, shows that although her public profile was of strength to the point of toughness, even though some of the language is political in tone, and she was deeply committed to Nelson. We become aware not only of her ideology but also of her awe – and love – of Nelson Mandela's greatness and humanity.

I returned in the early hours of today after almost three sad weeks of the most emotional storms in our life of separation. I however had one thing to look forward to, the letter from you which I knew would make my year. I knew it would reconstruct my shattered soul and restore it to my faith – the nation. Moments of such self-indulgence bring shame to me at such times when I think of those who have paid the supreme price for their ideological beliefs. Some of those fallen ones were dearer to me than my own life.

The letter was there, dated 4.2.85. I'm rereading it for the umpteenth time. Contrary to your speculation at first, I do not think I would have had the fibre to bear it all if you had been with me. You once said I should expect the inevitable fact that the struggle leaves debris behind; from that moment those many years ago I swore to my infinitesimal ego that I would never allow myself to be part of that political quagmire.

If life is comprised of the things you enumerate and hold dear, I am lost for words due to the fact that in my own small way life feels a little more monumental, material and demanding of one's innermost soul. That is why the love and warmth that exude from you behind those unkind concrete grey monotonous and cruel walls simply overwhelms me, especially when I think of those who in the name of the struggle have been deprived of that love.

You refer to moments when love and happiness, trust and hope have turned into pure agony, when conscience and sense of guilt have ravaged every part of your being. It is true, darling, I've lost so much of what is dearest to me in the years of our separation. When you have lived alone as I've done as a young bride and never known what married life is all about you cling to minute consolations, the sparing of one from the indignities that ravage us . . .

[From: *Part of My Soul* by Winnie Mandela, edited by Anne Benjamin, adapted by Mary Neson (Penguin Books 1985) copyright Rowohlt Taschenbuch Verlag GmbH 1984]

Her reverence contrasts completely with the great journalist and writer Martha Gellhorn, who shows how she coaxed the great ego that was Ernest Hemingway out of a fit of sulks.

In January 1940, Gellhorn wrote the following to Hemingway, then her husband, after returning from a separation of some months while she was reporting from Europe and he remained at their home in Cuba:

I, the undersigned, Mrs Martha Wasp Fathouse Pig D. Bongie Hemingstein hereby guarantee and promise never to brutalise my present and future husband in any way whatsoever, neither with weapons nor pointed instruments, nor words, nor uncalculated sudden phrases nor looks . . . I promise equally to cherish him, and not only cherish him so that I know it . . . and that I also recognise that a very fine and sensitive writer can not be left alone for two months and sixteen days.

[From: *Martha Gellhorn: A Life* by Caroline Moorhead, Chatto & Windus, 2003]

The Lebanese poet and artist Kahlil Gibran was 21 and penniless, living in New York, when he met Mary Elizabeth Haskell, ten years older than him, and the headmistress of a fashionable girls' boarding school in Boston. They became friends and corresponded regularly but it was only after Gibran's death that it became known how close the two friends were.

[Boston]
[Spring 1912]

What are you writing – and how does it go? And what are you thinking about – and how does it go? And what do you want to talk with me about? – and how do You go?

And why aren't your arms six hours long to reach to Boston? And what old canvasses have you been painting over? And when will You come to me in a dream and make night sweeter than night?

Mary

[New York]
Sunday, March 10, 1912

Mary, dearest Mary, how could you in the name of Allah, ask me if my seeing you gives me more pain than pleasure? What is there in heaven or earth to inspire such a thought? What is pain and what is pleasure? (Could you separate one from the other?) The power which moves you and me is composed of both pleasure and pain, and that which is really beautiful gives nothing but delicious pain or painful joy.

Mary, you give me so much of pleasure that it is painful, and you give me so much of pain too, and that is why I love you.

Kahlil

[New York]
Saturday, June 17, 1922

Beloved Mary,

God has given me much through you. How blessed it is to be one of God's hands. And how fortunate, how much more than fortunate, I am to know that hand, and to touch it, and to take from it. It is so good to be a little willow on the bank of a great river.

May God bless you, beloved Mary. And may His sweet angels be with you on sea and land.

Love from
Kahlil

[From: *Beloved Prophet: The Love Letters of Kahlil Gibran and Mary Haskell and Her Private Journal*, edited and arranged by Virginia Hilu, Barrie & Jenkins, London, 1972]

It's clear from all these letters that lovers need to reassure one another that they are well and safe and wish their partners to be so too. They seek reassurance that feelings have not changed, and that their overtures are still as welcome. There is the delicious idea that these correspondents could not have been so fluent with anyone else. Only with their loved one can they truly open their hearts, and often this marvellous person inspires and fortifies them against the troubles of life. We are therefore intruding a little on their privacy.

Chapter summary

- It enriches relationships if you can find a way to let your friends know that you care about them
- With family and friends you can have fun, enclose tokens and items to amuse them, and be creative
- In a love letter, sincerity is all. Just express what you feel – but avoid rhyme
- If the words don't flow, take quotes from literature, poetry, song lyrics

10
Making Your Complaint Letter Count

10.1 HOW DO YOU COMPLAIN?

It's important to keep calm. Few people know how to complain well. It's a skill like any other and most people do it badly, probably because they haven't thought the situation through. The problem occurs mainly because we complain when we are cross. Our anger can range from general dissatisfaction at something irritating but basically trivial, to white-hot rage because of faults which damage us, the people we care about or the state of the world. We believe that some person or organization has let us down, short-changed us, misunderstood us or damaged us and the things we hold dear – and we wish for a measure of redress.

It's interesting that when you look up the words *complain* or *complaining* in the dictionary or thesaurus, the associated words are all negative: at best we have words relating to legitimate protest, but at the other end of the scale they go from grumbling, whining, carping, nitpicking and finding fault, to being unreasonable, bad-tempered, belligerent and disagreeable. This is because so many people understandably use complaining as a vent for their anger. Indeed it always helps to get something off your chest, but it may not achieve the end result you desire.

If what we seek is an apology or remedy for some wrong, is a display of anger the most appropriate way to obtain those ends? While not suggesting that you avoid displaying your displeasure entirely, might not another route be more effective?

Dr Elizabeth Kubler-Ross, who worked with people who were terminally ill, produced a famous graph of human reaction to any negative news. The Kubler-Ross curve can be applied to all kinds of scenarios, and may well be applicable in some of the instances which lead us to complain. It goes like this:

- shock ('this cannot be happening!')
- disbelief or denial ('it can't be true!')
- anger
- depression ('that's the last straw! Why me?')
- acceptance
- action

This tells us nothing more than that anger is part of a process of emotion when we are thwarted or upset. To isolate it may not be wholly constructive. It may indeed have the negative effect of making the recipient of the complaint defensive or even hostile. In the latter case, you could wind up with a major war of words and precious little else.

We may feel the need of vengeance, yet it probably only brings temporary satisfaction. Usually the wrongful deed is done, and probably cannot be undone, so what you really require is that the perpetrator acknowledges their error, says sorry and makes amends.

If we accept that there's little to be gained by backing the target of our complaint into a corner, let's see what can be done to achieve our aims of an appropriate apology and redress.

10.2 WHAT ARE YOU COMPLAINING ABOUT?

Complaints generally fall into one of the following groups:

Goods
This is something you have purchased: an item or product, a holiday, travel ticket, a meal or even a property. In this instance, it is probably worth checking your rights before you make your approach. This way, you will know precisely what you might expect by way of redress. There are all kinds of legal acts and arbitration organizations which govern every aspect of consumer purchase. For instance, if you are buying products, your rights at the time of writing will be covered by:

- The Consumer Arbitration Agreement Act
- The Consumer Credit Act (where credit is extended. This includes credit cards)
- The Consumer Protection Act
- The Sale of Goods Act
- Trade Descriptions Act
- Weights & Measures

These acts are constantly being improved and updated. Many of them appear in a concise and easy-to-understand form on the Internet on an excellent website which is part of the Office of Fair Trading (www.oft.gov.uk). You can also seek advice from Consumer Direct which works in partnership with local authority trading standards services and can be contacted on 08454 040506. Alternatively, you could visit the Trading Standards Central website (www.tradingstandards.gov.uk). On the latter site, you will also find a list of advice sheets which cover problems with goods and what your rights are relating to distance selling regulations – shopping from home or on the Internet.

For holidays, if you have purchased a package trip from a reputable travel company, you can consult the Association of British Travel Agents (ABTA). New legislation is currently mooted about compensation for air travellers, which airlines will have to comply with. Meals in restaurants and cafes, and food generally, are covered not only by the Consumer Protection Act but also the Food Safety Act. New homes are covered by the National Home Builders Council, which sets minimum standards for builders of new properties.

Services
These can range from a painting and decorating job in your new kitchen to failure to read the electricity meter or a poor maintenance job on your car. Utility companies have regulatory bodies and, should the company fail to respond to your complaint, you can take the matter further by contacting the appropriate body.

Currently, telephone companies are governed by the Telephone Ombudsman, OTELO; gas and electricity supplies are regulated by energywatch (the Gas and Electricity Consumer Council), and water by the Office of Water Services (OFWAT).

With less regulated services, you can probably gain help from Consumer Direct which works in partnership with the Trading Standards Services (for instance by referring case details of scams and dishonest traders so that appropriate action can be taken). Their advice sheets cover problems with motor vehicles, including second-hand purchase, repairs and servicing.

Professional services

This covers professional negligence of some kind, most frequently relating to either health or legal services but can also cover insurance, banking, architecture and surveying. All these areas may be daunting to anyone who is not well associated with them. However, all are well regulated and complaints are dealt with scrupulously and very seriously.

Health/Medicine

Possibly the best place to start with any complaint relating to health is the NHS Patient's Charter, which gives patients' rights regarding health care provision by GPs, hospitals, community services, ambulance services and dental, optical and pharmaceutical services. Copies can be found on the Internet (www.pfc.org.uk/medical/pchrt).

In the first instance, complaints concerning general practitioners, GP out-of-hours cover, dental treatment and charges should be directed to the Family Health Service Authority. Complaints relating to hospital treatment should be made initially to the chief executive of the relevant hospital trust. You can also seek advice from the Patient Advice and Liaison Service (PALS) which has offices in most major NHS trusts.

More serious complaints against doctors can be made to the General Medical Council, which licenses doctors to practise in the UK. It will consider complaints against doctors and has the power to prevent any offending doctor from practising. Dentists are regulated by the General Dental Council. There is also an Ombudsman for Health known as the Health Service Commissioner, but you must have taken your complaint to the relevant health authority before you can consult at this level.

Legal matters

Any legal complaint is usually directed at a solicitor. This may range from concerns about a solicitor's fees to incompetent advice or work.

The main path of recourse is the Consumer Complaints Service at the Law Society (www.lawsociety.org.uk or phone 0845 6086565), which will investigate the complaint and will make contact with the offending solicitor on your behalf. There is also a Legal Services Ombudsman but this office can only be consulted where there is no positive result from the Law Society.

Others

Complaints relating to surveyors can be directed to the Royal Institute of Chartered Surveyors, and those relating to architects to the Royal Institute of British Architects.

Banks have clear codes of practice and the head offices of major banks usually have a complaints procedure for their customers. Should this not be effective, there is a Banking Ombudsman. There is also an Ombudsman for Insurance but, again, this approach is only valid if you have found the complaints procedure of the insurance company unsatisfactory.

Local problems

One of the main complaints about neighbours – and this can mean a local pub, cafe or club as well as other householders – is related to noise. Fortunately nowadays, noise is seen as the disruptive 'pollution' that it is, and most local councils take a tough stance on this kind of nuisance and have a special department with daytime and out-of-hours phone lines for complaints. Some residents experience problems over nearby or adjacent gardens. Here your Citizen's Advice Bureau may be able to guide you, if a friendly word over the fence has failed. Antisocial behaviour issues with neighbours may be in the province of your community police officers, if direct appeals for peace do not work.

Local and national government

In matters relating to education, planning, local amenities, housing, roads and so on, and to aspects of national government policy, one of the routes of complaint is via your local politicians. We look at letters to local councillors and MPs in Chapter 12.

Having boned up on your rights, you now have to decide how serious a complaint this is and what level of approach is appropriate.

10.3 SMALLISH SINS

It's a slip-up, a genuine mistake, hasn't done vast damage but you still feel that someone should know about it, or make good, or both. It may be a product – a pair of shoes, bottle of wine or a washing machine – or a service, such as plumbing (the pipe still drips), an endless wait in the supermarket queue, or car park ticket machines that have broken.

When you purchase a product you have legal rights under the Sale of Goods Act and other appropriate acts as described earlier in this chapter. However, before you bring all that into play, why not allow the shop, salon, gallery or supermarket the opportunity to sort it out amicably and courteously? You could pay them a visit or telephone them in the first instance. Only if you have failed to meet the right person or obtain the desired reaction may you need to put it all in writing.

Large organizations will usually have a section that deals with consumer complaints, usually called customer service or customer liaison. If this is the case, address your letter to the manager of that section. If possible, obtain his or her name by phoning the switchboard, and use it in your letter. For smaller companies, write to the managing director. Even if the MD doesn't handle complaints personally, his or her secretary will be able to redirect them to the correct person.

The form of your letter should be fairly matter-of-fact. After all, the person who opens and answers your letter is probably not the actual culprit. Where a complaint is not serious, it may even help to give your letter a certain lightness of tone – you may achieve a much better and quicker response.

Even so, assemble all the necessary information, and be sure to date your letter. The sequence is:

- When (and if appropriate, where) did the problem occur? (e.g. *On 13th October, I purchased a pair of grey high-heeled shoes, price £80, at The Store, High Street.*) Give a code or reference number, style name and manufacturer's name and description if you have them.

- What is the exact nature of the problem? (e.g. *I bought the shoes for a family wedding and wore them only on this one occasion. Halfway through the event, the sole split apart from the upper, and the shoe was then useless.*)

- What happened as a result of the problem? (e.g. *My partner had to miss part of the reception, because he had to drive home and find me another pair of shoes. They didn't match my outfit and I felt both cross and very inelegant!*)

- Spell out what you would find acceptable by way of recompense. Do you seek just an apology, or a refund, or an assurance that new practices will be put in place, or some other kind of action? Do you require financial compensation or the replacement of the goods or services? Whatever it is, express what you believe to be a reasonable response.

- Where appropriate, give a time period within which compensation/amendment would be acceptable.

Case study

For several years, I worked in the publicity department of a well-known drinks company and took part in setting up its consumer complaints service. However good and immaculate the bottling lines, and scrupulous the supervision, there were rare instances when things went wrong and something peculiar went on the shelves in error. One such instance was some dry cider in a returnable bottle. All the complaint letter said was: 'Thanks for the raffle tickets. Have we won the prize?' and in the accompanying bottle, almost hidden by the labels, were two little raffle tickets suspended in the liquor. Obviously, someone had put their old raffle tickets into the empty bottle on its previous trip out. When the bottle came back into the factory, somehow the washers had failed to wash them out, and the scanners didn't catch them either. So the bottle was refilled, tickets and all, and sent out again.

But the letter was fun, so we decided to be fun back. We wrote to announce that they had won not only our profound apologies for the loss of cider and the inconvenience, but also, yes, a lucky prize. We sent little bottles of calvados (the cider liqueur), a pottery wassail mug, some chocolates and a generous supply of replacement dry cider, all dressed up in cellophane and ribbons. In due course, we received a happy thank-you note.

Other examples
Whatsits

Mr Greaves
The Manager
The Accounts Department
Wotnot and Whatsit
Birmingham B. ...

27th July 20—

Dear Mr Greaves,

Your Invoice No: G/W&W/9043

I received an invoice, number as above, dated 18th May 2004, for 18 dark green Whatsits purchased from your company by mail order at the end of April. I duly paid the invoice on 27th May, with a Lloyds TSB cheque number 1000061. The cheque was clearly received by your company because it appears on my June bank statement as redeemed on 1st June 2004.

Unfortunately no one informed your computer which is now churning out increasingly bright red and inflamed demands on a fortnightly basis. Please could you switch it off?

Yours sincerely,

Charlie Hearthrug

PS The Whatsits are perfect.

Bedlams

40 Prisms Approach
London N. ...

Mr Lauda
Bedlams Nightclub
42 Prisms Approach
London N. ...

6 November 20 —

Dear Mr Lauda,

I am genuinely pleased that your nightclub is so immensely popular. Unfortunately, we your neighbours have a problem. My wife and I also enjoy a night out but sometimes find it impossible to accomplish because our car has been barricaded in by your revellers' vehicles. We've tried all the usual please-don't-park-here, 24-hour-use signs but to no avail.

Is there anything you can do to help us? Since we are virtually next door to Bedlams perhaps your security man could direct cars away from our drive. We simply have to find a way around this. I don't really want to have to call the police and have the cars towed away but, when I can't get out, I become so mean spirited that I'm tempted to do just that! Please could you arrange something before next weekend?

Yours sincerely,

Andrew Sinclair

10.4 EXPERT ADVICE

Tony Northcott FTSI is a Trading Standards Consultant and spokesman for the Trading Standards Institute. He says:

> I have five golden rules when writing letters of complaint:
>
> - try to make sure your letter is sent to the right person or department;
> - try and keep your letter short;
> - be polite (sarcasm or rudeness are out!);
> - say what you want for your complaint to be resolved, and
> - give a reasonable timetable for action.
>
> Most importantly – always keep a copy of the letters you write.

10.5 WEIGHTIER SINS

Your first letter brought no response or one which was unsatisfactory. Alternatively, your complaint is about something that has caused considerable damage, or has caused you to lose time from work in order to deal with the implications, or has given you extra expense, and no doubt has created a great deal of stress for you.

A second letter should be to the highest level of the company or organization. Detail the initial complaint. Be explicit: give the date and place of any purchase, an accurate description of any goods or service, with the manufacturer's name and any code or reference numbers, and the price you paid. If you are complaining about a service, describe what the worker was asked and expected to do, what they actually did, how long the procedure took and, if appropriate, whether the work was checked.

Then outline the lack of response to your complaint. It should be a clear statement of what happened, with the dates, times, names of people contacted, plus the reaction or lack of it.

This can be followed by a short, sharp list of the current problems and the implications the problem has had for you. You should include a concise note of any expenses incurred, and any lost work time or loss of income. You can also state that the incident has caused you considerable stress and disappointment.

You may also wish to point out the implications of further non-response. You can point out that, should the matter not be resolved to your satisfaction, you will have no alternative but to appeal to the relevant authority, e.g. regulatory body, trade or professional organization or even to your MP or a solicitor. This should elicit a reply. If it doesn't or it is unsatisfactory, you may have to follow through by contacting the appropriate higher authority.

Always keep a copy of your letters and send them by recorded delivery. List any phone conversations you have had, noting the names of the people you have spoken to and the dates of your calls. You will require this documentation if the matter has to be taken to a higher level.

Example

Albert Street, Droitwich, Worcs

The Water Authority

21st October, 20—

Dear Sir,

On 28th September I wrote to the Customer Care Department regarding the level of service received; a copy of my letter is enclosed.

On Wednesday, 1st October my wife received a phone call acknowledging receipt of my letter and that I would shortly be receiving a letter from a manager. The next day I myself received a phone call saying that the matter was being dealt with and I would be shortly receiving a letter concerning my complaints from a manager. To date I am still awaiting a reply.

This I find totally unsatisfactory. To recap:

- On 29 September an engineer arrived to investigate our flooded basement. He informed us that in his opinion it was not sewage and that I should contact the District Council but he did take samples away for analysis. This was despite the fact that our inspection chamber had started to fill up. Even an inexperienced person would know that the problem was the sewer. I have yet to receive results of the water analysis.
- On Tuesday, 30th an engineer called next door – their basement was also flooded – and he discovered a blockage in the main sewer. In the meantime we

received a call saying that an engineer would call on Wednesday. I phoned to say that the matter was rectified. The engineer still arrived the next morning.

I am certain that you would acknowledge that there are serious weaknesses with your procedures. Please would you provide me with a written reply to the following:

(i) An explanation for the failure to provide a written explanation to my original letter. (This surely contravenes your Code of Practice of responding to complaints within 10 working days.)

(ii) As to when I will receive the results of the water analysis (your Emergency Call Centre announced that I would receive them within two weeks).

(iii) Why three engineers are sent to deal with one problem and why one arrived after the blockage had been cleared.

(iv) As to why no advice is given regarding the clearing-up after having sewage in your home.

(v) What the Water Authority is going to do to prevent this happening again. It appears that the blockage caused water to leak where pipes are bolted together and that the remedy is to plastic-line the old iron pipes.

Finally, as a fault of flooding lies with the Water Authority, I understand that I am entitled to a refund of your sewerage charges. Could you please confirm this.

Yours faithfully,

D. G. Crawley

[reproduced with kind permission of David and Sheila Crawley]

10.6 COMPLAINTS AGAINST *YOU*!

Supposing it is *you* to whom a complaint letter is sent. Perhaps someone has just cause: the roots from the tree in your garden have undermined their patio, your offspring did indeed have the music at a mega-level the night you were out, the paint you used in a work job did peel, the repair that you undertook has failed. Maybe the complaint is debatable. Either way, you must now respond.

Occasionally, that's it, you have made a real howler and nothing can retrieve the situation. In the majority of cases, I believe that a complaint well handled can give you a good neighbour, friend or customer for life. If you own up, take responsibility for whatever has happened, do everything you can to rectify the error, people will respect you for your honesty. More, they know they can trust you in future to respond well if there are any other problems.

However you decide to handle the matter, do it quickly. If you cannot resolve the issue right away, respond immediately with a phone call or letter, not just apologizing but also reassuring the recipient that you will be taking action within the shortest possible time.

I suggest that you give people the space to be angry. We live in a time-pressured society and inefficiencies or disturbances cause yet more stress. Once people know their complaint has been heard, most reasonable people will calm down, particularly if they know you are going to work with them to sort the problem out.

It can be quite hurtful when someone accuses you

of something that you do not consider to be your fault. But, occasionally, someone might be totally unreasonable. You know it and possibly they are aware of it too. However, before you box their ears, consider how this might affect future relationships. Will it create a negative atmosphere in the area in which you live or work? If so, consider if it would be wiser to set aside full fairness or justice, and take the wider view. This means handling their complaint as though it was legitimate, although you may wish to gently outline the true facts of the issue. Alternatively, you may be dealing with a bully, in which case succumbing without a fight may be counter-productive. In this instance, standing your ground, firmly and with courtesy, may be the best policy.

In all other instances, the best form is to deal with the complaint in the way you would wish it to be dealt with were you the one complaining.

Example

The Garden Centre, High Street, Coreham, C.. ...

Mr & Mrs Appleby,
57 Waverley Grove
Coreham

8th April 20 —

Dear Mr & Mrs Appleby,

Your Order for Indian Slate Paving Stones
Our Sales Ref No: GC1069

On behalf of The Garden Centre, I would like to apologize very sincerely for the incorrect ordering of your paving slabs. The mistake was entirely ours and was down to a lack of attention to detail; it was a silly mistake that could have been prevented if the assistant had been more thorough when completing and processing the order. I am truly sorry for the inconvenience this has caused you, and assure you that the assistant has been taken to task over this matter.

We have now reordered and expect the paving stones of your choice to arrive within the next four to five days. We will then deliver them at your convenience and collect the incorrect ones.

We will also be sending you with our compliments a small ornamental tree, which we hope will grace the new paving area when it is laid.

Yours sincerely

Shirley Keating
Manager

Larchway, Tree Lined Grove, Woodlands WD9 4HH

7th October 20—

Dear Anita,
I am dreadfully sorry that I left my car blocking your driveway on Sunday. You have every right to be furious with me. I am at a loss to explain how I could have been so thoughtless. I was in a rush to change because David was picking me up, and I just didn't take enough care.

Is there anything I can do to make amends? Trim your hedges?

Wash your car? Actually, I am not being flippant; I really can't apologize enough and I promise that it will not happen again.

From a very repentant,

Chloe

Chapter summary

- Try not to make your complaint merely a vent for your anger
- Remember that the person you are complaining to may not be the real culprit
- Give dates, places, times, code and reference numbers, product descriptions, and the exact nature of the problem
- State clearly what you would find acceptable to resolve the issue
- If you are not sure what your rights are, check with the relevant legislation or governing organization
- Always keep copies of correspondence
- If there is a justified complaint against you, own up and be honest in your wish to make amends

11
Charity Appeals

GIVING TIME, ENERGY, MONEY

Increasingly, many benefits in our society and our communities are brought about by charities or groups of volunteers coming together and giving their time and energy as well as money. It may be that you know of a charity that for personal reasons you wish to raise money for, or possibly there is a need within your local area: the church desperately needs a new roof or organ, the local hospital would benefit from a special kind of scanner or an air ambulance, or the old people's club would relish a summer outing or Christmas party. Somehow you have found yourself on the fundraising committee and you have been asked to organize the appeal for funds.

Alternatively, you may be organizing an event or running for a favourite charity in a marathon, or you are planning an expedition to climb a mountain or hike across deserts. In order to fund the trip properly, you will need at least one sponsor, and it is up to you to find them.

Professional charity fundraisers break down their campaigns into 'cash and kind'. They know that support comes in different forms, the main ones being:

- *A donation of money.*
- *The gift in kind.* This might be a piece of equipment, goods to raffle or sell, or someone's expertise or time working on your behalf.
- *Sponsorship.* You may be seeking a lot of sponsors – for a sponsored walk, run or climb – who will pay up when you have accomplished your feat. Or you may be looking for a commercial sponsor who will underwrite your expenses. In this instance, unlike someone who is just giving a donation, the sponsor is looking for an association – usually in the form of publicity (see page 195) – with what you are doing.

See what sort of support is most suitable for your fundraising appeal. It may be just one kind of support or even a mixture. The approaches would therefore be slightly different.

11.1 DONATIONS

If the organization you are raising money for is a registered charity, don't forget about Gift Aid. Anyone who is a UK taxpayer wishing to make a donation, be it large or small, regular or one-off, to a recognized UK charity, can use Gift Aid to increase its value. The charity can claim the tax from the Inland Revenue and add it to the balance, and this currently adds 28 per cent to the value of the donation (for more information about this, visit www.allaboutgiving.org).

If this applies to your fundraising, you may wish to add a Gift Aid form to your appeal letter. See an example opposite.

11.2 WHO TO ASK

If you are responsible for creating the mailing list, as well as the appeal letter, there are various points to consider.

- Large national companies are targeted by hundreds of charities all the time. If you live close to the head office of a major company and lots of their staff live in the area, it is still worth approaching them. But just be aware that everyone writes to Richard Branson and Bill Gates!
- If yours is a local appeal, you may well do better to approach local companies, or the nearest branches of well-known supermarkets who often have local appeal funds.
- If your appeal letter lands on the wrong desk, it may not automatically be passed on to the right one. It may be well worthwhile to invest some time in phoning the company you are targeting and asking for the name of the chairman or managing director, or, in the case of a very large company, ask for the name of whoever handles their charity donations. If the person on the switchboard doesn't know, the publicity or human resources department should do so.

Example of a Donation and Gift Aid Form

Donation & Gift Aid Form
(name of charity)

My Full Name: _____

My Address: _____

_____ Postcode: _____

Telephone Number: _____

I would like to donate (please tick)

☐ | ☐ | ☐ | ☐ | ☐
£5 | £20 | £50 | £100 | other (please specify)

Please make cheques payable to (name of charity)

Gift Aid Declaration

Sign this Gift Aid Declaration and every pound you give to (name of charity) will increase in value by 28p, helping your contributions go even further *(see notes below)*

I would like (name of charity) to treat the following as Gift Aid donations *(delete as appropriate);*
- The enclosed donation of £ _____
- All donations I have made since 6 April 2000, and all donations I make from the date of this declaration until further notice

Signed: _____ Date: ____/____/_____

Please return this form in the enclosed FREEPOST envelope or send it to: Name and address of charity

1. You must pay an amount of income tax and/or capital gains tax at least equal to the tax that the charity reclaims on your donations in the tax year (currently 28p for each £1 you give).
2. You can cancel this declaration at any time by notifying the charity.
3. If in the future your circumstances change and you no longer pay tax on your income and capital gains equal to the tax that the charity reclaims, you can cancel your declaration (see note 1).
4. If you pay tax at the higher rate you can claim further tax relief in your Self-Assessment tax return.
5. If you are unsure whether your donations qualify for Gift Aid tax relief, ask the charity. Or ask your local tax office for leaflet IR 65.
6. Please notify the charity if you change your name or address.

(reproduced by kind permission of the Cleft Lip & Palate Association)

- Many organizations support charity appeals: the Rotary, Lions, Masonic Lodges, even the Women's Institute make charitable donations. Many sports organizations, from football to golf, select a Charity of the Year. So do some business people's associations such as PROBUS. Write and ask early enough and your appeal might benefit.
- Local solicitors may know of local trust funds. These are trusts set up by local benefactors to aid specific purposes, sometimes for the disadvantaged, or for training and education or for buildings and facilities. Write to local solicitors' practices and ask if they know of any such trust funds.
- There is likely to be a higher response where an organization, company or individual has some affinity with your appeal. We all tend to do this. If we have family or friends who have been affected by a certain kind of medical condition, for instance, we are more likely to give generously to the charity that helps patients or supports research into that illness.

11.3 YOUR LETTER FOR DONATIONS

Be very clear about what you are asking for. If your appeal has a title, use it in the heading of your letter, or use it immediately after the greeting. Explain precisely:

- what the appeal is for
- why the appeal is necessary
- your timescale
- the target amount

- how the money will be spent
- who will benefit

Explain who you are and your qualification for asking for the money (for example, secretary of the appeal committee or volunteer charity fundraiser). If your organization and its aims are not well known, briefly give some background about what it does and how it helps in the community. If your organization has a charity number, ensure that it is displayed on the letter heading.

Keep the initial letter short but offer to supply any further information or references that may be required. Always include a correspondence address and a phone number, preferably a daytime number.

11.4 EXPERT ADVICE

Julia Smith, who is a professional fundraiser, and has worked for the British Lung Foundation and Joint Action, which raises money for orthopaedic surgery research, suggests:

You need to be a raspberry ripple in a sea of vanilla! It is important to remember that, whether you are seeking support from charitable trusts, national or local business, or individuals, your appeal is one of many that are likely to be received. You need to bring your appeal to life and make it stand out from the others as much as possible. Here are a few ideas:

- Start your letter with a quote from a service user that endorses the need for the service and how it has helped them. Remember, you will need to outline how the quote will be used. The person may wish to be referred to as Mrs RB from Croydon rather than being named in full.

- Include interesting statistics.
- If you are raising funds for school or playgroup equipment or facilities, you could consider attaching a picture drawn by a child to illustrate the need.
- For raising larger sums, research is the key to success. The more information you have about your potential donor the easier it will be to match the donor to your appeal. Mass mailings simply do not work. Your efforts are more usefully put to targeting your appeal to those most likely to be interested.
- Your strongest chance of success will come from approaching warm potential donors, with whom you have a link. Use your own contacts to see if they have any links with your list of potential donors. They could open the door for you with a preliminary phone call to say that you will be approaching them and that your appeal is important.
- In your appeal letter, make reference to any specific knowledge you may have and try to link it to your appeal, for example, 'Knowing of (company name)'s involvement with xxx I thought you might be interested in how we are proposing to xxx'.

In conclusion, use your imagination to bring your appeal to life. If the potential donor is able to share your vision they are likely to want to be involved with the project's success.

Gareth Davies, director of the Cleft Lip & Palate Association, adds:

Most potential funders like to know what efforts have been made to secure funds from other sources. They will be more keen to match support from others than to commit themselves as sole funders. For instance, a local residents' association may already have clubbed together and put in x per cent of the cost of a new after-school facility and local companies might be invited to make up the difference.

Remember, too, that it can sometimes be more effective to break an appeal down into its component parts. For example, instead of asking for contributions towards the total cost of the new facility, it might be more attractive to funders if you highlight specific items that they might consider funding. Your request might be set out as follows:

The total estimated cost of the new facility is £5,000. This is broken down as follows:

New bathroom suite:	*£1,500*
Heating and wiring costs:	*£2,000*
Furnishings:	*£1,000*
Paint/décor:	*£500*

By giving funders a choice of what they might like to contribute to, and by specifying amounts, you may well find your overall target is more easily reached. Take care, though, to ensure you don't end up with too many pledges of support for the same item! Your initial letter should give people a choice but also make it clear that if there are any shortfalls elsewhere, their donation may be diverted to cover these. You might also choose to adapt this technique for 'help in kind' approaches. You could, for instance, target a local DIY store for paint and décor, a local plumbers' merchant for the bathroom suite, a local furniture shop for help with furnishings and so on.

11.5 YOUR LETTER FOR GIFTS IN KIND

Some organizations may find it difficult to give you a donation, but they may be able to help in other ways. You can even give a 'shopping list' in your letter. For example, you might write on the lines of:

> We are seeking help in any one of the following ways:
> - a prize for our Christmas raffle
> - advice on setting up our accounts
> - any second-hand computer equipment
> - a venue for our monthly committee meeting. We wondered if we could use the room in your staff sports club complex.

Some companies make staff transport vehicles – minibuses or coaches – available to charity organizations, along with a company driver, for special events. Others may donate goods or supplies. When a new hospice was being built in Cornwall, the trustees were thrilled to accept the donation of many tonnes of concrete and hard-standing, delivered on site and duly laid by a local company.

It's not only the large companies that are willing to help; small ones may do so too. Bakery shops will sometimes make a special cake; an electrician will donate a few hours of expertise, the haulier will pick up a part-load, the solicitor might make particular introductions, and local celebrities might add their name as an endorsement or come along to boost a special event.

The message here is that if you don't ask, people can't say yes.

Examples

The Manager
The Garden Centre
Garden Road
The Downs
Truro
TR. ...

23 March 2005

Dear Manager

Although we are very aware of the generous support you already give to local charities each year, I am writing to you on behalf of St Julia's Hospice, Hayle, and Mount Edgcumbe Hospice, St Austell, to enquire if you would kindly be willing to help us in our vital work by donating a prize, perhaps a gift voucher, for the Hospices' Annual Christmas Draw which will take place in December this year.

Our two Cornish Hospices operate as two separate charities under a common Board of Trustees, and both provide special-ist palliative care to people who are affected by life threaten-ing illnesses. The work our doctors, nurses and other multi-disciplinary professionals undertake brings comfort to many affected by these diseases and helps in the relief of pain and other distressing symptoms. All the services we provide are free of charge and are based only on need. As the Hospices receive only a very small percentage of their income through the Health Authority, they are heavily reliant on the generosity of the local community and people such as yourselves to help us to continue to provide care and comfort in Cornwall.

Together the two Hospices need to raise in excess of three million pounds every year to secure their future and your support would be a very positive step towards this.

With best wishes,
Yours sincerely

Linda Knight (Mrs)
Fundraising Assistant

[reproduced by kind permission of The Cornish Hospices]

Mr Major Funder
Major Funder
London
EC. ...

28th January 20—

Dear Mr Funder

Further to our conversation last week, I enclose some details of our work at Cleft Lip & Palate Association with the hope that we may benefit from this year's Charity Day in December.

As you know, our Patron is Carol Vorderman, whose brother

was born with a cleft lip and palate. She has let me know that she would be delighted to represent CLAPA on the day.

The funds raised on the day will make a huge difference to CLAPA's work. In 2001 we received £150,000 from GMTV's 'Get Up and Give Appeal'. With this funding we were able to commence several much needed projects for children and teenagers born with clefts, including confidence-building children's camps and a magazine for the same age group (9–15). These projects have proved so successful that they have become part of our core services.

We have not benefited from a large injection of funding since 2001, and know that if accepted, we could put in place badly needed projects; amongst others, to develop our services to children and increase the general public's knowledge and understanding of the condition.

I have enclosed some literature, giving examples of our current service provision. Please call me if you would like further information about cleft lip and/or palate, or about our work at CLAPA.

Yours sincerely

Dan Mars
Fundraising Officer

Enclosures: CLAPA News 2004, One in 700 leaflet

[reproduced by kind permission of the Cleft Lip & Palate Association]

SPONSORSHIP

11.6 INDIVIDUAL SPONSORSHIP

There's a slightly different emphasis with sponsorship. If you are undertaking a sporting event or feat of endurance for a specific charity, you will probably want to ask your employer and local companies, clubs and any organizations you belong to, as well as all your family, friends and colleagues, to support you.

Always tell the charity well in advance what you plan to do. The charity may already have sponsorship forms, T-shirts, collecting boxes and so on that you can use. Some of the bigger charities offer places in the London Marathon and hold a reception for their runners after the event. This gives you a chance to meet the charity, have a place to meet your family or supporters, eat, drink and even see a physiotherapist to ease those sore calf muscles.

If you are writing a letter to gain this kind of individual sponsorship, be sure to explain why you are attempting whatever feat of endurance it is, the amount of money you are hoping to raise, and some details about the charity you are supporting.

By and large, these sponsors will not expect any acknowledgement, although it is courteous to ensure that they are properly thanked when you have completed your task and collected their money. Most people like to know how you got on, how much money you have managed to collect overall and how the money was handed over.

11.7 COMMERCIAL SPONSORSHIP

This is the kind of sponsor who will underwrite some or all of your costs in return for some kind of publicity. The art of effective commercial sponsorship is to find a business that is in some way complementary to your organization or appeal or event, and offer ways that will put the sponsor's name in an appropriate way in front of potential new customers.

You can seek either an overall sponsor – in which case the whole event will bear the sponsor's name – or break down your requirements and seek lots of smaller sponsors. Let's consider some examples:

- If you are raising money by climbing Kilimanjaro or taking a bike ride in China, try approaching local insurance agents as well as travel agents for support.
- If you are running a charity fashion show, you could approach local hairdressers to donate the models' hairdos and a raffle prize of a session at his or her salon.
- One local charity organized a cookery demonstration, with the chef of a local hotel and products from all the local delicatessens and bakeries, which promptly gave discount vouchers away at the same time.
- If you are organizing a sale in support of your local school, approach bookshops, computer shops and stationers for suitable items.
- Sometimes, exhibitors at county shows or local exhibitions will allow you to run a raffle from their stands.

Work with a potential sponsor on the publicity element. Unless it is entirely inappropriate, suggest that their name is featured prominently, for example the display of a poster or flag with their name on it.

If there are programmes for the event, confirm that their contribution will be acknowledged and offer free advertising space. They might require an advert in the programme of an event, their name on your T-shirt, the side of a vehicle or a banner, or to have their company's name as part of the title of your event.

Examples

Tristan Vanhegan
London N. ...

1st April 2004

Dear

I'm taking part in the London Marathon 2005 on 17/04/2005 to raise funds for Leukaemia CARE Society and would really welcome your support.

My training is coming along fine and I've done far better than I was expecting in the Silverstone Half Marathon and the Kingston Breakfast Run (16 miles). I hope it all continues to go in the right direction. A while ago I went to a Gold Bond holders' conference and was told lots of good tips on diet and nutrition, preparation, what to expect on race day, etc. One bit of good news is that they've replaced the cobbled section this year, which has caused a lot of anguish in the past.

Leukaemia CARE was my choice and I want to raise as much

as I can for them. Last year my ex-girlfriend Sarah's cousin was diagnosed with leukaemia and told he did not have long to live. However, with excellent treatment and support he defied doctors' expectations and is now in remission. He is able to live at home once again. It was a very difficult time for all of Sarah's family and I would like to raise money for a charity that has already made significant headway in treating this disorder.

Please do your best to sponsor me. It's really easy – you can donate online by credit or debit card at the following address:

http://www.justgiving.com/tristanvanhegan

All donations are secure and sent electronically to Leukaemia CARE Society. If you are a UK taxpayer, Justgiving will add an automatic 28% bonus to your donation at no cost to you, making it worth even more. Please join me in supporting Leukaemia CARE Society and a fabulous cause!

If you activate the link above you will get my marathon web page and can see both a photo of me and how I'm getting on with my sponsorship!

Best wishes,

Tristan Vanhegan

[reproduced by kind permission of Tristan Vanhegan who, with an original target of £850, finally raised £2,100 by his marathon effort. He says that 80 per cent of his supporters used the email method of giving.]

Mr Potential Sponsor
The Garage Group
Head Office
Cornwall
TR. ...

7 March 2005

Dear Mr Sponsor,

In October 2005 Mount Edgcumbe Hospice, a registered charity, will be commemorating 25 years of providing specialist palliative care to people in the local community who are terminally ill. To mark the occasion we will be holding an Autumn Ball in the beautiful grounds of Boconnoc House, just outside Lostwithiel on Saturday, 17 September 2005. We will be having a celebrity after-dinner speaker, an auction, and live band.

Invitations to our 25th Anniversary Ball will be extended to businesses and individuals in the community as well as the local media who wish to support this excellent local charity. It is our intention to hold the ball as an opportunity to commemorate the important milestone in Mount Edgcumbe Hospice's history, but with the aim of raising £25,000 towards the work of the organization.

We are seeking the support of Cornish companies who may wish to help in some way and I have drafted some ideas as a support package. I wonder if you could give a few minutes of your time to consider the attached proposals.

I would be happy to come along to discuss these in more detail at a time convenient to you and will telephone you in the next week to see if you are interested in giving your support.

I appreciate that you probably receive hundreds of requests every day from charities and organizations. We try not to ask for support too often; however, we do feel our 25th Anniversary is a very special and important occasion. We hope you will consider supporting and sharing it with us.

If you feel the attached options are not suitable, but you may be able to assist in other ways, I welcome your suggestions.

Yours sincerely
Sarah Snell
Head of PR and Fundraising
Mount Edgcumbe Hospice

And here is the company support package Sarah supplied:

Support Package for 25th Anniversary Appeal

Option One
Company to sponsor one course of a four-course dinner for 250 guests.

A specially designed 25th Anniversary Menu will be produced for each guest and will highlight the sponsor's support and contact details. e.g. 'Roasted Seville Orange glazed Duck Breast with a Port and Wine Jus – The Garage Group has kindly sponsored this course.'

Tickets will list names of all our main sponsors. We will produce a series of press releases during the year about the anniversary, and all sponsors will be highlighted in this publicity. Local press, television and radio will be invited to attend the ball.

Maximum sponsorship per course £1,250
Maximum sponsorship of main course £3,750

Option Two
Company to sponsor drinks reception and canapés for 250 guests. Maximum cost of sponsorship £2,500 (£5 per guest). Alternatively, company to sponsor wines served with the meal. Maximum cost of sponsorship based on 100 bottles of wine @ £8 per bottle £800.

Option Three
We will hold an auction during the evening and would welcome good quality prizes with a perceived value of at least £50–£100. Examples: A round of golf and lunch; a candlelit meal for two; a weekend break; a crate of wine; a day at the races; a balloon trip; National Trust family membership; paint balling; a trip on the London Eye.

[reproduced by kind permission of the Cornish Hospices]

Chapter summary

- Appeals can be both for cash donations and gifts in kind
- Be precise about what you are asking for, why the appeal is necessary and how the money will be spent
- Explain who you are and, if possible, use the registered charity number
- Sponsorship differs from donation; commercial sponsors may require publicity or acknowledgement
- If you are organizing a sponsorship event, tell the charity about your plans

12
Writing to Politicians

12.1 COMMUNICATE WITH YOUR REPRESENTATIVE

Our democratic system is founded on the right of every person to be duly represented at parish, district, national and EU level. This means that when you feel strongly about some issue or problem which affects you as an individual, or something in your locality or relating to the state of the nation, it is your right to have your opinion made known and, where appropriate, your interests represented to the governing authority.

There are a number of ways in which you can communicate with your politicians. Members of Parliament (MPs), for instance, will hold regular weekly or even twice-weekly 'surgeries' in their constituencies where you can meet them face-to-face, either by appointment or by going to a drop-in session.

Many people prefer to write. This has two advantages: it gives the writer time to set out the problem clearly and logically, and attach any necessary background material, and it also gives the politician, whether at local or national level, time to assess and maybe even research the issue you are concerned about before he or she replies.

It is important to understand that party politics should not play a part in the representation you can expect. If, for example, you are a fervent socialist and your councillor, MP or MEP (Member of the European Parliament) is from another party, this should not affect his or her willingness or ability to represent your interests.

Where there is an issue about which many people take sides, it will strengthen your argument if others who share your views also write in. This will help your representative assess how widespread the concern is, or how much importance is being attached to a local matter. The numbers of letters will count.

Often people say they will write in but somehow they don't get round to it, or find they don't have all the information they need. If the issue is complicated and the arguments are diverse, it may encourage your friends and neighbours to write if you create a standard letter, containing all the relevant facts and figures, as a basic guideline, so they can then personalize it in a letter of their own. This personalization is important. Politicians – and council officers – can see when a letter is too obviously a 'form' to which people merely add their address and signature, and they tend not to take them quite so seriously.

However, it is worth remembering that sometimes resources will be allocated in a different way solely because of public reaction. For example, if enough letters are received by a local council from people who feel strongly that the amount of chewing gum on pavements is unacceptable, it damages dogs' paws and is unsightly and unhygienic, then resources may be made available for pavement cleaning in the next round of budgets.

On more serious issues, politicians will find the backing of letters helpful in verifying the views and general mood of electors. Politicians work in conjunction with civil servants and council officers, and solid proof of public reaction has real value in some issues.

Sometimes it is difficult to decide to whom you should write. In general, the breakdown is as follows. District and borough councillors are responsible for education, the provision of schooling and further education; roads, relating to parking restrictions, congestion charges, traffic wardens, maintenance, signage and speed controls; planning; street cleaning; safety in the streets and public areas; parks and leisure (libraries, sports centres); housing, and some social services matters.

Health, the police and emergency services and the armed forces have their own governing authorities. However, where there are matters which spill over into public safety or are of national concern, you may wish to write to your MP.

MPs are responsible for public policy and the strategy behind all our services, such as health, environment, agriculture, and so on, as well as issues of national security. A good constituency MP will take heed of local matters – and local opinion – because they may well be a reflection of a larger picture and therefore affect national policy. They will welcome informed opinion from experts on aspects of national concern. Certain large-scale local matters will concern MPs, such as the proposed closure of a major hospital or a major development within their constituency.

MEPs represent their British constituents at European Parliament level. Here, their remit is the policy on Europe-wide issues such as agriculture, fishing, trade and trading standards. Often the implementation of the legislation is a matter for each member state. However, many MEPs are willing to intervene when there are cross-country issues, such as someone who has worked for a Dutch company for many years and finds that their pension rights are being infringed, or someone who has bought into a time-share property in Spain, and finds there's a dispute between a builder and landowner. Although an MEP does not have any power in such issues, he or she may well give advice or write to the local council, mayor or notary on a constituent's behalf.

12.2 THE GROUND RULES FOR LETTERS

- You don't need to explain what your political affiliation is: this is irrelevant.
- Politicians won't mind if you handwrite your letter, but ensure that your writing is legible. Space the lines to make it easy to read. Use wide margins.
- Be as brief as possible, remembering that politicians – or their staff – may have to work their way through dozens of letters every day.
- For the same reason, state the point of the letter

right at the beginning. You can also give the letter a title line to highlight its subject.

- Give all the necessary references. If, for example, you are making a point about a planning application and you have the reference number, write it clearly at the beginning of your letter. Add the address of the development too.

- If the property or issue is in another country, and you are approaching your MEP to write to an overseas official on your behalf, it is helpful to have the names, exact titles and addresses of the officials.

- Do not be over-emotional; instead present your facts and figures, and your logical conclusions. To say, for instance, that a development is ugly may well be true, and you may feel very strongly about it but in fact this is only a subjective reaction. Therefore, this element is not one that the council authorities take into account when granting or refusing permission. There are indeed features that may be taken into account, such as loss of sunlight or view, but by and large decisions are not based on sentiment or aesthetics.

- Try not to use your letter merely as an outlet for your anger. Be polite. Your passion for the issue will still come through.

- If your letter is forwarding information, rather than a request for help, it is useful if you clearly write 'For Information' at the top of your letter.

- Check your spelling and punctuation.

- Finally, don't forget to print your name clearly and include the date, your address and all your contact details. This should be done even if you are sending your letter by email, because it helps the politician to establish that you are a constituent.

12.3 EXPERT ADVICE

Jenny Kingsley is a Liberal Democrat councillor in the Royal Borough of Kensington and Chelsea. She says:

People find me via the council's website, my newsletters, at local residents' meetings, or even through their local library. I receive about 70 per cent of the communications by email and, if there's a major issue, there may be dozens in a week.

I read them all, so it helps if the letters are well presented. Local councillors, unlike MPs, don't have any staff, but I reply to every communication, even if it's only a postcard to thank them for the information or to say that I will be looking into the matter. Most of the letters I receive are relevant, although I sometimes have to work out whether the correspondents are merely writing about their pet gripe, or whether there is a real issue. A smattering of letters would be better directed to an MP, and one or two are from lonely people who are perhaps full of anger and pain and are using the system as a form of therapy. Those are the hard ones to respond to. I also receive telephone calls from residents about all sorts of issues.

Many residents complain that councillors don't answer or acknowledge their correspondence. The whole point of being a councillor is to provide local representation. If you don't receive a reply from your councillor in a reasonable time, I recommend that you send a tactful reminder. You can always phone. If you still don't have a response,

I suggest that you bear this in mind when it comes to the next election. Use your vote; it does send a message!

Some people don't use the system because they feel unable to write, either through a lack of educational or language skills or from a lack of confidence. If you find writing this kind of letter very difficult but you feel strongly about an issue, why not seek help? Voluntary organizations may well assist you: try the local law centre, Age Concern, Citizen's Advice Bureau or Sixty Plus group. You could even ask for help at the local school or college – young people, teachers and staff may well be flattered to be asked.

Steve Pound is Labour MP for Ealing North. He receives about 250 emails and an average of 40 to 50 letters per day at the House of Commons, sometimes up to 100 in the busiest time of the year, which tends to be in the winter. There is further correspondence resulting from the twice-weekly surgeries he holds in his constituency.

There's no substitute for a hard-copy letter: it's a commitment, a statement, in a way that emails are not. Someone who has taken the trouble to write to me deserves an answer and I try to reply to everyone. Even schoolchildren writing in receive a personal letter; it's a way of encouraging them. Sometimes I receive aggressive or even abusive mail, either on a personal level or from people having a go at the government, but we thank them anyway for making their views known!

Quite a lot of correspondence results from people copying me in as their MP. It's a common mistake. People will be writing to their council about a local issue, and think their letter will have more impact if the MP knows about the problem too. Or they write to me in the first instance and I pass it on. In fact, occasionally there is an interface between local council and national governmental matters. In my constituency, this could be issues around the proposed additional runway for Heathrow or something relating to the A40. By and large, MPs have to be generalists when it comes to their constituency and I find it immensely valuable to have experts – people who really know what they are talking about – writing in to me.

There are several ways to attract my attention. Establish any previous connections: for instance, if you have met me, do mention it ('We met last year at . . .') or if you want to know my views on an issue, I will have to respond. I'm less likely to reply to someone who spells my name wrongly.

Sophie Hosking is Steve Pound's parliamentary manager. She spends about 90 per cent of her time handling his correspondence. She adds:

I help to filter and sort the mail that arrives by post or fax. The shorter the letter, the better. My heart sinks when there are pages of packed writing. We don't mind handwriting as long as it's clear. I don't dislike emails either because it's quickfire, and makes it easy to go back to people if we need further information, but they do tend to be more abrupt. A title is useful, or an outline of what the letter is about in the first paragraph. Sometimes I read a letter and at the end I still don't know why the person wrote to us!

Daniel Hannan is the Conservative MEP for South East England. He keeps in contact with his constituents via regular emails on subjects which may affect them, or about which he feels strongly. He also has a regular column, 'At the Heart of Europe', in the *Sunday Telegraph*.

I receive a large volume of junk mail, including, for some reason, annual reports from various organizations such as universities and councils, none of which is relevant to my role. However, I always reply if someone has bothered to write me a letter. Then there are the organized letter campaigns, some of which are on Euro-specific issues. One of the most successful campaigns related to an EU proposal to restrict certain high-dosage vitamins and herbal remedies. I received over 5,000 letters – not postcards – objecting to the proposal. While I could see that there had been some kind of template, every letter was individual. It was a highly focused campaign, and what made it so good was the timing and that each letter explained precisely the action the correspondent wished me to take.

It's very important to write to me in good time, when the policies are being formulated and discussed, not after the legislation has been passed.

About 40 per cent of my correspondence relates to some actual or perceived violation of human rights. This is an area of confusion which is almost universal: the European Court of Human Rights has nothing to do with the EU Parliament. Instead it is connected to the 43-member Council of Europe, a completely separate institution. Since the Human Rights Act, some of the sillier cases tried in the European Court of Human Rights have received a lot of media attention, and so people see this as a route to solve all kinds of grievances.

As a result I now have a standard letter to redirect people.

Dear (Constituent),

The European Court of Human Rights is a court in its own right and works separately from the European Union or its court and institutions. I am therefore not in the best position to help you with your question and I suggest that you get in touch with the court directly so that they can advise you on the admissibility of the case you mentioned. The court only comes into play when a plaintiff has exhausted the national courts.

Information about the European Court of Human Rights is available on the court's web site (www.echr.coe.int) and you can also telephone the ECtHR in Strasbourg directly on 00 33 388 41 20 18.

Other examples

The following letter is very long, but it has been included because it contains many of the relevant points you could use when objecting to a planning application.

Dear Mr ———

Re: DPS/DCSE/PP/03/01504/BC South Kensington Underground Development

As a resident in the immediate locality, I am writing to you to object to the most recent proposals for the redevelopment of South Kensington Tube Station, and the adjacent properties in Thurloe Street and Pelham Crescent.

While I am in favour, in part, of the first proposals made by [developers' name], their second, most recent plans are not suitable on the following grounds:

1. The site is in the Thurloe/Smith's Charity Conservation Area which consists mainly of early Victorian buildings, many of which are listed buildings. Thus, the design of the buildings is not in keeping with this historic area.

2. The proposed twelve-storey office building will tower over the neighbourhood and will dominate this at present beautiful region. It will be an unwarranted intrusion on the skyline, particularly bearing in mind the immediate proximity of our national treasures, the Victoria and Albert and Natural History Museums.

3. Neighbouring properties will suffer loss of daylight and sunlight as a result of the tower height.

4. Local residents will have to endure three months of sleepless nights while builders put a top on one of London's last open air tube stations.

5. At present, the shops in the station complex provide a vibe to the area, and a fulcrum with a strong sense of community in South Ken. The present proposals would not allow these small shops back in. In their place would be impersonal supermarkets. This is not acceptable.

6. The scheme provides for 180,000 sq ft of offices and retail space and 125 houses. Vehicular access to the entire scheme is to be taken from the south-west corner of Thurloe Square, where access is already difficult. The proposed scheme will thus have an adverse effect on those who live in the area and who require access. It will also pose a threat to pedestrians.

7. The area surrounding the site is already very congested. There are long traffic queues frequently in Exhibition Road and Thurloe Street; Pelham Street is also often congested. All of these streets have bus routes. The proposed development of residential, office and retail accommodation will attract considerably more cars and large vehicles on a daily basis and thus increase congestion and pollution. This situation will have a marked adverse impact on the quality of our local environment.

8. The scheme does not provide any affordable housing, on or off the site.

9. There is minimal outside space.

I ask that the Council refuse to grant planning permission to this second proposal for the development of South Kensington Tube Station.

Yours sincerely, etc.

18 Melthorpe Lane, Pembridge PM6 1TE

Mr S Mapleton MP
House of Commons
Westminster
London SW1 0AA

7th March 20—

Dear Mr Mapleton,

Changes at Pembridgeton Hospital

I am writing to you about the proposed changes at Pembridgeton Hospital. As you may know, it is suggested that all major waiting-list surgery is transferred to Waylands Hospital, and this will mean that the Intensive Care Unit, rehabilitation and physiotherapy departments, and the relevant clinics will also be moved.

We understand that services in the NHS must be streamlined and run as economically as possible, but there does not seem to be a specific reason to justify this upheaval. Waylands is 25 miles away, so the impact is likely to be felt throughout this community. My concern is on three levels:

- The Operating Theatres: Those at Pembridgeton recently underwent extensive and expensive refurbishment. Will this now go to waste? The operating theatres at Waylands are not so 'state-of-the-art'.
- Transport for Patients: The majority of the population is elderly and many are waiting for joint replacement operations. In this rural area, they would be dependent on local transport to attend appointments and physio, and as you know, bus services are infrequent. This lack of transportation would also make it difficult for elderly friends and relatives to visit partners/family members in hospital.
- Accident & Emergency Facilities: It is unclear whether the A&E department will also be moved. If so, may I point out that Pembridgeton is the closest hospital to the motorway, with its occasional pile-ups, and the town centre with its regular Saturday night rowdies. However, it also makes a nonsense for surgery and the Intensive Care Unit to be on separate sites from A&E.

I appreciate that these changes are as yet 'under discussion', but I believe that you should be aware of the acute concerns of your constituents. Of course, I am also petitioning the Regional Health Authority as well.

Yours sincerely,

Maudie Asquith

Chapter summary

- Party politics should not play a part in the representation you can expect
- On important issues, encourage other people to write as well
- If you handwrite your letter, ensure it is legible
- State the point of your letter at the beginning, and include any necessary reference numbers
- Always include your name, address and daytime telephone number in case the politician requires further information

13

Letters to the Editor and Agony Aunts

NEWSPAPERS AND MAGAZINES

It is a fundamental part of our democracy: the right of every citizen to make their feelings known publicly, that is, free speech either by demonstration or via the media. It is not just lip service; notice really is taken of the viewpoints that appear in the press. The Letters to the Editor page is traditionally very well read. Whole campaigns have been launched by a well-placed and emotive letter.

The drawback is that such pages are hugely over-subscribed. *The Times*, for instance, receives up to 500 letters in any one day, seven days a week, with about 80 per cent now sent by email; the *Observer* receives between 150 and 300 per week by letter and the same number again by email. They both only ever use on average about a dozen in each issue.

An editor putting these pages together is looking for a breadth of opinion, a measure of controversy and a degree of entertainment. It can help if you are well known already or a prominent member of any organization relevant to the subject being aired. However, if you are going to use the name of any organization, you may need to check that the opinion you express is subscribed to by the whole organization, rather than the personal viewpoint of just one member.

Newspapers and magazines also like genuine wit. For many years, the last letter on *The Times* letters page has been either very funny, very clever or both.

13.1 CHOOSING THE PUBLICATION

Your first decision is what publication you wish your letter to appear in. If you want to comment on a specific article, or respond to a previously published letter from someone else, it would be natural to write to the publication that the article or letter has appeared in. If the issue raised has been published in a specialist magazine, but has importance to a wider audience, you may wish to approach a more general publication, referring of course to the original. For example, you might address a letter to *The Times* or the *Daily Telegraph* with a line such as *A letter which appeared in* The Lancet *of 23rd April raises the issue of the poor quality of autopsies requested by a coroner. This has wide implications with such cases as the GP Harold Shipman* . . .

Where you are initiating the subject, you will want to select the publication where you have the highest chance of your letter being published and where the greatest influence can be gained. It doesn't always have to be a national newspaper; you may find that you will have more impact elsewhere.

If the issue has international implications, or was raised in the UK Parliament, or in a programme on national television, you may even consider writing to several publications, although in this instance it may be appropriate that you also have several versions tailored to each one. No newspaper likes printing letters seen in all the others.

Overall, the general guidelines are:

- International/national issues: national daily and Sunday newspapers.
- Regional issues: regional daily newspapers, county magazines.
- Local issues: local weekly newspapers, parish magazines and local property or general interest magazines.
- Professional issues: professional and trade journals, company and staff magazines, national media where the general public may be affected.
- Specialist interest: specialist magazines (from bird watching to civil rights, travel to football).

Health and social issues might also be of interest to women's magazines; comments on transport matters may have impact in motoring organizations' magazines.

This country has a wealth of publications on every possible subject, some being subscription only, but most being on general sale. If you don't know what publications are available in your area, or relevant to your field of interest, consider a trip to your local reference library. They will probably keep copies of local newspapers and magazines, as well as the national dailies. They will also have media directories which list all national, local, professional and trade, and consumer press. These directories will also give you the postal and email addresses of the publications and the circulation figures.

Where there is time, try to obtain a copy of the newspaper or magazine and check the letters pages for style and length. To increase the chances of your letter being selected, consider not only what you want to say, but how you will write it.

13.2 BREVITY

Look closely at the letters columns of the journal you want to write to. Count the words. Are you surprised at how few words there are? The selected letters will have been professionally edited; there will not be a single spare word. Hopefully the editor will have done this without losing the sense of the original. Newspaper training makes for this kind of hard, very tight writing. 'Foot pedal is a word too long,' one of my newspaper editors used to say. Quite right – if it's a pedal you are referring to, you would only use a foot to move it. Foot is therefore a superfluous word.

You may not feel equipped to write so tightly. It is a skill that takes time to learn. However, you can ensure that you make your point as succinctly as possible. For example, consider the following sentence:

In my opinion, this road scheme will have the effect of increasing traffic rather than decreasing it.

That's seventeen words. In fact, we can say the same in just nine words – and also make it a stronger statement. Firstly, we can delete *in my opinion* because it doesn't add to our knowledge; we already know that's what you will be expressing. The sentence might therefore read:

This road scheme will substantially increase, not decrease traffic.

One of the ways to edit your own work is to write it, put it aside for an hour, then look at it again to see what can be taken out without spoiling the sense. Read it aloud. Can you make it sound stronger and more positive? If you are using a computer, another trick is to put the text into a type face and type size that you don't usually use. It makes it look different and somehow you can see what you have written more objectively.

13.3 SUBJECT MATTER

Take another look at the letters pages. Note that most of the letters deal with a single point on any one issue. This is particularly true of national newspapers and magazines. Decide what is the most important point you wish to make, and express that first and in the strongest terms. If there is an equally strong second point, add it in. You have nothing to lose, but don't be surprised if that is the part that is sacrificed to the demand on space.

Most local newspapers and some academic journals

may allow you more space, where you can express your views in more depth and expand the number of points you wish to make.

13.4 REMEMBER THE READER

If your letter is published, remember that every reader of that publication will form an opinion of you, based on the view you are expressing. Before writing you should be very sure that you are happy to express your views before everyone you have ever met. It is possible that former teachers, old boy- or girlfriends, current colleagues, business rivals, family, friends and neighbours may read it. It is sensible, in light of this exposure, to ensure that you won't feel embarrassed, intimidated or irritated by any feedback from people you know.

13.5 YOUR NAME AND ADDRESS

Always include your name, address and a daytime telephone number, even if you wish them to be withheld from publication. The newspaper, magazine or journal will need to verify that you are indeed the author, and that the letter isn't some kind of malicious practical joke.

13.6 TIMING

As in so many aspects of life, timing is all. If you wish to respond to something in the national daily media, you will have to do so quickly. Few issues last more than two days. Your letter has far more chance of being considered for publication if it arrives in time to be printed in the following day's issue. Remember, national newspapers receive hundreds of letters and only feature twelve to fifteen. Early birds stand a greater chance of being read by the letters page editor. This is where email comes into its own. All our national newspapers will accept letters by email and usually flag up the appropriate email address of the letters page prominently.

Regional daily newspapers work on the same time span. Weekly papers usually have the letters page as 'early pages', that is among the first to be completed, leaving the news pages until last in case situations change or more urgent news comes in. If your local paper comes out on a Thursday ensure that your letter arrives by the first post on Monday morning.

Magazines differ. Weekly women's magazines work about four to six weeks in advance; monthly magazines – professional, specialist interest and general – work from two to three months in advance. Some specialist and professional magazines, if weekly, work only one week in advance. The best way therefore to find out the deadlines for submitting your letter is to phone up and ask.

13.7 EMAIL

If you are sending your missive by email, take care with the subject field. As Stephen Pritchard of the *Observer* points out, their email address, in common with many thousands, gets bombarded with all manner of commercial junk. A clear title – including the legend Letter to the Editor – helps the staff sort welcome wheat from irritating chaff.

13.8 EXPERT ADVICE

Stephen Pritchard, readers' editor of the *Observer*, has written a column advising people how to increase the possibility that their letters will be noticed. He says:

> We have guidelines set out every week on the letters page but it's amazing how many people ignore them. The rules are simple: Don't start your letter 'So'. Be brief: never more than 300 words. Stick to the point. Be legible. We don't mind handwritten letters but the letters' editor can sometimes feel like a pharmacist faced with scores of illegible prescriptions. Oh yes, and avoid green ink.
>
> It's worth noting that the letters which stand the most chance of success are those that take an issue forward and throw new light on a subject. Those that merely disagree with a point in the paper or complain and carp without substance to their argument usually get short shrift.
>
> This may make you feel that letters are unwelcome. Not so. We need to hear your ideas and opinions. We have an open policy here. All staff have access to Letters to the Editor, both in paper and electronic form. They are widely read, so even if your letter isn't published, you can be sure that many people here will have seen it.

['So you want to write to the editor', Stephen Pritchard, the *Observer*, 03/02/02. Copyright Guardian Newspapers Limited 2002]

Andy Simpson, readers' letters editor of the *Daily Mail*, which receives about 400 letters a day and publishes about 40, adds:

> Brevity and relevance are important but we here on the *Daily Mail* cherish one thing in particular – opinion informed by experience. Either one, without the other, is a less interesting read.

Sample letters
From the *Evening Standard*

Real Mums Squeezed Out
Helen Morrissey CEO and mother of six is reckoned to be one of a new breed of 'Alpha Women', a successor to Eighties' Super Women who really can have it all (15 June). But rather than admire her energy, I think she has an easy ride. The yawning gap between her life and ordinary women is that she has staff (and a stay-at-home husband) allowing her to fit in yoga sessions while they do the jobs most mums take for granted.

A lot of working women I know lead busy lives, and still find time to sit on committees, make cakes for school fairs and be with friends and families without awestruck respect from the media. Morrissey is lucky to earn a six figure salary, but what would be important for me is the amount of time I could give to all my children and my husband.

C Hamblet, Tonbridge

17 June 2005

From the *Daily Telegraph*

International ID needed

SIR – Whether ID cards cost £300 or 3p (report 17 June) they are worthless unless they can be interpreted throughout the world, as well as being proof against forgery.

Terrorists and villains are infinitely mobile and only international ID cards have any chance of being effective. Perhaps the UN could take the initiative with a bit of prodding from world leaders, who might be expected to foot the bill in their own best interests.

Duke of Buccleuch
Bowhill, Selkirk
18 June 2005

From the *Independent*

Teaching children the skills they need

Sir: I was fascinated by the proposal that we should 'set aside time' to teach youngsters such skills as letter-writing ('Teenagers with GCSEs lack basic skills', 29 June).

In the days when English GCSE was examined by the 100 per cent coursework method, one English faculty included a work-related module. The students wrote letters of application for jobs, constructed their CVs, filled in application forms and wrote covering letters to accompany them and then role-played job interviews. We even had banks of interconnected telephones on either side of a wall dividing two classrooms so that we could simulate them telephoning a large company to confirm arrangements for an interview. After the mock interview, they had to give feedback to each other and write an evaluation, stating whether they would have given the candidate the job for which they had been interviewed.

We don't do this any more because we don't have time. But it was a very valuable exercise.

So, fine, let's change the syllabus to accommodate such skills once more, but, please, don't let anyone run away with the idea that it's new, or that it was the fault of teachers that such opportunities were axed. It was a political move.

VAL HARRISON
Birmingham
1st July 2005

From the *Daily Mail*

Olympic Spirit

School playing fields are certainly important (Mail) but when I attended Stratford Grammar School in East London, where the 2012 Olympics will take place, we didn't have a playing field at all.

Despite this, our head girl, Jean Disforges – who went on to marry Ron Pickering – represented England in the hurdles event. She used to train in the school corridor!

If the urge to win is there, any problems can be overcome.

PATRICIA MARRIOTT (née SAMUELS),
Romford, Essex
14 July 2005

And, traditionally, the last letter is always amusing:

From *The Times*

Humans Welcome

From Miss Christine Moulié

Sir, A friend of mine sent a fax to a hotel in the French

Pyrenees, asking if his dog would be allowed to stay at the hotel. The reply was to the effect:

I have been a hotelier for 25 years. I have never seen a dog steal an ashtray or a spoon, or burn sheets with a cigarette. I have never had to call the police for a dog being drunk and disorderly and a dog has never been rude to the staff. That's the reason why I always welcome dogs.

PS You too are welcome, should you decide to accompany your dog.

Yours faithfully,

CHRISTINE MOULIE

Queensgate Place, NW6

August 24

ADVICE AND AGONY AUNTS

The advice column is another accepted part of our culture. Advice columns in magazines and newspapers range from the highly practical – gardening, motoring, law and DIY – to medical (alternative as well as ortho-dox medicine) to the highly charged and emotional agony columns.

The guidelines for the more practical advice are much the same as writing any letter to a newspaper: be succinct; keep to one main point, in this case your question, and ensure that your letter fits the magazine or newspaper you are sending it to.

Agony columns play a slightly different role, even though the letter writers are not identified. There is an element of 'counselling' that means that agony aunts must be particularly sensitive and responsible, at the same time being aware of what will entertain all the readers of their pages. The agony aunts I talked to when researching this chapter said that the majority of their correspondents start their letters with the sentence: 'I have never written to an agony aunt before.' The 'aunts' are also aware that once someone has written out their dilemma, they are often part way to a solution.

In her hilarious book, *Dear Mariella* (Bloomsbury, 2004), about her Sunday newspaper advice column, Mariella Frostrup says: 'It's as if the mere process of confronting your concerns can provide a glimpse of an answer ... The very act of scrutinizing what is making you unhappy and then giving it form, whether verbal or written, is part of the process of change. It won't pay off your mortgage, or turn your wife into a sexual bobcat or bring back your husband, or reunite you with your sister, or stop your boyfriend from stashing porn under the bed, or cure your loneliness, or make your mother start taking responsibility for her life. It will force you to open your eyes to the possible causes and the potential solutions. I may have just written myself out of a job.'

13.9 EXPERT ADVICE

Corinne Sweet, a trained counsellor, psychologist and life coach, as well as an established self-help author and agony aunt, takes up this point:

Writing to an agony page is part of the healing process, or rather, the beginning. It is often a first step towards acknowledging and owning a problem, even though most people know that the agony aunt or uncle will probably not reply personally. The act of voicing something, in print, which is painful, shameful or troubling, can be a way of beginning to tackle a greater life change.

Writers to agony columns should be aware that their letters will be publication fodder to some extent. Editors are always desperate to have a large, genuine postbag covering a variety of issues. However, the pressure of deadlines and lack of resources usually means only a few letters, say six or eight, are chosen and edited down for publication. Run-up times to publication can also be painfully long, a matter of weeks, even months, before a reply may appear.

I urge any potential agony letter writer to seek as much help as possible, even while just contemplating writing a letter. It may help to write a letter; however, if in need of talking to someone anonymously, the Samaritans are always there, twenty-four hours a day. It is no stigma at all to call them as they provide a wonderful, confidential listening service and can provide some instant relief from pressing worries and cares. A visit to the GP may also help, as they may refer on to a free counsellor or therapist. Similarly, other organizations, such as Relate, Cruse Bereavement Care, Parentline Plus and the British Association for Counselling and Psychotherapy can provide names of counsellors and therapists in a writer's local area. There are also helplines available, which can often be found in a local telephone directory or by a quick trawl of the Internet.

The main thing to remember when writing to an agony column is to think carefully about what you reveal. You have no control over what may or may not be published, so don't write anything you wish to keep private. Also, keep a letter short and to the point. Of course, if a letter writer wants complete anonymity because of the sensitivity of the subject, they need to make this clear to the editor when writing in.

See Further Information, page 249, for contact details of organizations mentioned by Corinne Sweet.

Chapter summary

- Respond quickly – preferably by email – to a daily newspaper
- Select the publication you write to with care. Sometimes local papers or specialist magazines will have more impact than a daily
- Be succinct – eliminate all spare words
- Decide the most important point you wish to make and emphasize it
- Always include your name, address and daytime telephone number to verify your authorship
- You can write to an agony aunt if you have a problem, but consider the implications of publication before you post it

14
Common Mistakes, Spelling and Other Howlers

14.1 AVOIDING MINEFIELDS AND BEAR-TRAPS

People who become fluent in English as a second language are very impressive. We have an enormous vocabulary; lots of rules on structure, with endless exceptions to those rules. There are many words that look the same but sound entirely different – for instance, say out loud: *cough, bough, dough, rough, through, borough* – and there's another group which sound the same but have different spellings, for example, *paw, pour, poor, pore*. Lots of words have been acquired from other languages, and then there's all those home-grown colloquialisms, proverbs, quotations, references and buzzwords. It's a challenge and fascination even to native speakers.

By and large we are a literate nation, but the sheer wealth of the language means that there are minefields and bear-traps when it comes to compiling the perfect letter. It's therefore only sensible when you have to write an important letter to invest a bit of time in ensuring that it is as correct as you can make it. There are very strong reasons for this: it establishes that you are literate, thoughtful and committed; it is a courtesy to the person you are writing to, and it makes it easier for him or her to read. Errors have a way of tripping the eye and making the reader go over a sentence several times to make sure that they have understood. If people have to read a lot of letters – newspaper letters page editors, HR people, politicians and so on – it is an irritant when there are glaring mistakes, and it can mean that the strong points you may be making could lose their power, and your letter might not be taken seriously.

As suggested earlier, if you are not a regular and fluent letter writer, one worthwhile measure is to do a draft copy. Set it aside for a while. Look at it again later to see if and where it needs amending or correcting. Only then consider setting out the final presentation. Unless you are very sure that your punctuation, spelling and sentence structures are spot on, it is good practice to ask someone you trust to read it through for you. Four eyes are always better than two.

If there is something that you are unsure about and you don't know how to check, look at the sentence to see if there is not another way of writing it. There often is. Invest in a good dictionary. Because our language continues to grow and change, with new words appearing or becoming fashionable, and other words dropping from use, it is worth buying one every few years, or using the most up-to-date dictionaries in the local library. Meanings change, so do spellings and usage. For example, my mother would refer to another woman as *dainty* or even *refined*. We don't use those words in that way now; only oil is refined! I come from the *laid-back* generation which sadly disappeared some years ago in favour of something more stressed: currently kids strive to be *cool*.

If you regularly write letters and reports, you may find it useful to invest in a thesaurus which gives you lists of alternative words. Many computers have a thesaurus built in as part of the software but, as a professional writer, I find these very limited and rather unimaginative compared to, for instance, *Roget's Thesaurus*. A couple of guides to English usage and one on titles and forms of address may also prove valuable.

14.2 PAY ATTENTION TO STRUCTURE AND STYLE

The structure of your letter

Consider who you are writing to. Do they require a short formal letter or a longer explanation? If the subject is a very lengthy, complicated one (for example, to your local councillor about a major planning matter in your area), should you present it as a very long letter, or would it be more acceptable as a shorter letter with the background information attached?

When you read your letter back, try to see it through the recipient's eyes. Will the reader understand immediately what the crux of your letter is? Other than for personal correspondence, most recipients will welcome it if you state the object of your letter at the outset. When appropriate, use a subject title after your salutation.

Young journalists are taught to write their stories in a pyramid: the top of the pyramid is the title (the point of the story, as it were), the next shortest section is the introduction which should hold the reader sufficiently to entice them to read on. This is usually the paragraph which outlines what the story is going to be about. More detailed information and explanations then follow to form the solid base of the pyramid. This same principle is worth adopting for various kinds of letters, particularly the more formal and business letter.

References

When you are writing a business letter – including a letter of contract or complaint – always include any reference numbers, codes, full names and descriptions of products and services, and place them on the page prominently.

Date

As discussed previously, you should always date your correspondence, and when in doubt use the old-fashioned form of figures and letters (20th July 2005). This avoids any confusion which may arise from using numbers only (20/7/05), since other countries use them in a different order from the UK.

Spelling

Don't rely on the computer spell-check. Use it by all means but remember, your computer will not pick up when, for example, you wanted the word *of* but you have written it by mistake as *if*. Both are spelled correctly but the use of the wrong one may make a nonsense of your sentence. Sometimes the software will not recognize a word you have used. This may not mean the word is incorrect, it may just be that your vocabulary is superior to the computer's. There's no way around this; you simply have to double-check the piece yourself.

Dictionaries are still a good investment. Every home and office should have one, the larger and more comprehensive, the better. When in doubt, check it out.

A list appears on pages 244 to 247 of the more commonly misspelt words.

Abbreviations

This is one of my pet hates. Some people think it shows how clever they are if they use lots of abbreviations for the organizations or even the job titles they are referring to, irrespective of whether or not the recipient of the letter knows them. This is infuriating and wastes the reader's time trying to work out what the letters stand for. The more formal the letter, the fewer abbreviations should be used. If you do use an abbreviation, it is only courteous to be sure that the recipient of your letter will instantly recognize what it means.

Capital letters

We use capital letters less than we used to. At one time you would write about the 20th Century. Now, unless you are referring to the film company 20th Century Fox, you would write it as 20th century.

The basic rule is that you only need use a capital letter for a proper name, place name or title, but not for general descriptions. For example, capital letters are required for: *Vienna, Kings Cross Station, the Royal Opera House*; but not for: *a capital city, a railway station, an opera house.*

North, south, east, west, central, greater don't require capital letters unless they are part of a proper name: for example, *in Central London, Greater Manchester, North Cornwall.* Dates – days and months – do require capitals, so do all public holidays and religious events. Holy books and religious leaders and their churches or institutions require capitals – and, not least, so does God and all His many and various names in all faiths and forms of belief.

If you are using an abbreviation, you would use capital letters but probably not with full stops between them – for example: *PM (Prime Minister), A&E Department (Accident & Emergency Department), BT (British Telecom).*

Sentences and paragraphs

Long and complicated sentence structures are just that – long and complicated. Unless you are drafting a legal document, where very precise language and descriptions are essential, keep your sentences short and to the point, particularly for business communications. Again, this aids readability and lessens the likelihood of misunderstandings. If you must use a longer sentence, check your punctuation carefully to guide the reader through it.

Dense blocks of writing, either printed or handwritten, look intimidating and off-putting. You can use paragraphs – of two, three or four sentences – to divide up your pages. Usually, each paragraph introduces another topic or a different aspect of the main theme. They aid both presentation and the reader's understanding. Paragraphs can be indicated in several ways. They can be shown by a gap between blocks of sentences. Another way is to indent the first line.

Punctuation

Reading a letter which has little punctuation can leave the reader breathless. Punctuation provides signals for the points within sentences and phrases at which there are the natural pauses that aid the reader's understanding. Punctuation tells us when there's a question, a quotation, a secondary point that you are making, or where there is a list.

Whole books have been written on this subject, and one became an international best seller. Don't be too intimidated, however. If this is an area of concern for you, try to keep it simple.

Our most common punctuation is:

. the full stop: used to finish a sentence.
, the comma: used to:
  – break up a long sentence to make it more readable
  – split off a phrase
  – break down a list
  For example:
  – *It is in everyone's interest if the reader is able to concentrate on the sense of what is being written, rather than being diverted by spelling mistakes.*
  – *Once upon a time, in a land far away, there lived a beautiful princess.*

– Now add the almonds, raisins, cinnamon and sugar into the mixture.

It's worth watching out for ambiguities. These can often be avoided by using commas correctly, for example:

– the manager said the customer was being rude.

Who was being rude, the manager or the customer? If it was the manager, you can use commas to show the meaning:

– the manager, said the customer, was being rude.

: the colon: used (as here) to introduce the explanation. It is also used to introduce a quotation. For example:
   – The mayor replied: 'We are delighted to welcome you to our town.'
; the semicolon: used to break up two sentences which are related but equal in strength. For example:
   – The paragraph is a useful way to break up a page; it aids understanding.
   – The princess slept for a hundred years; nothing in the Kingdom stirred.
"..." or '...' quotation marks: these are always used in pairs, in either the classic double quote marks style, or in single quotes. They are used exclusively to introduce a quote someone has made, or in reported or fictional conversation, to embrace the words said.
? the question mark: used to indicate a question. If the

query is within reported speech, ensure that the question mark is within the quotation marks.

- *The policeman asked: 'Is there anyone here with medical skills?'*

- the hyphen: used to link two or more words. It's easy to see that some words, including numbers, need a hyphen:

- *twenty-two, three-quarters*
- *up-to-date, mother-in-law*

However, hyphens are subject to fashion and the current mode is to use them sparingly. When in doubt, consult a good dictionary.

- the dash: can be used to split up a sentence, instead of commas or brackets. Dashes add pace to a sentence, introduce an aside, or give a span of numbers:

- *The mayor – a plump little fellow – rose to his feet and spoke.*
- *6.30–8.30 p.m.*

! the exclamation mark, like underlining, is used for very strong emphasis. It should be used sparingly. Use too many and you lose the impact and exhaust the reader's patience. One – or a maximum of two – can give a lift to a letter, when there's something exciting or dreadful to report.

- *It's true! We have a baby boy!*
- *You will never believe it; we've won some money on the lottery!*
- *The noise went on for* four *hours!*

Apostrophes

Apostrophes are also punctuation marks but are the cause of so much confusion that they warrant a heading of their own. It's because they are used in several distinct ways.

Possessive

Apostrophes give ownership. They announce that something belongs to someone or something else. The apostrophe stands in place of the word 'of' or 'belonging to'.

For example: *Cherry's book (the book of Cherry)*

This rule still applies even when someone's name (the name of someone) finishes with an 's'.

For example: *Thomas's book*

Possessive plurals

These appear more complicated, but hold firm! If you are using a plural word in its own right, such as men, women, children, people, a crowd, simply add the apostrophe as before.

For example: *It is within most people's grasp.*

It only requires attention in words which have an 's' at the end, such as animals, politicians, helpmates, friends. In this instance, the apostrophe follows the 's'.

For example:
- *It is within ministers' jurisdiction.*
- *He delivers the animals' food.*

Apostrophes are also used to take the place of a letter, and this has become more and more prevalent.

For example: *wasn't* (instead of *was not*), *hasn't* (instead of *has not*), *isn't* (instead of *is not*) *let's* (instead of *let us*), *they're* (instead of *they are*), *I'm* (instead if *I am*)

A very common problem area   The use of *it's* and *its* is one of the most common areas of error in the whole of the English language. The confusion seems to arise because they sound identical. There are other minefields: *who's* and *whose*, *you're* and *your*, *there's* and *theirs*, and not least *they're*, *their* and *there*.

The golden rule to remember is that the apostrophe takes the place of a letter, therefore:

IT'S (i)   *it's – means it is*
The apostrophe has taken the place of the 'i'.
For example: *It is raining: it's raining.*
           It is a problem: it's a problem.

IT'S (ii)   *it's – means it has*
The apostrophe has taken the place of the 'ha'.
For example: *It has been a long, tiring day: it's been a long, tiring day.*
           It has been a good harvest: it's been a good harvest.

ITS   The other form, *its*, is tight and possessive,
namely, *on its own, in its lair*.

The same applies to *who's* and *whose*. The apostrophe says where there's a letter missing, therefore:

WHO'S *who's* – means who is
        Again, the apostrophe has taken the place of the 'i'.
        For example: *Who is at the door: who's at the door?*
                     The man who is living over the road:
                     the man who's living over the road.

WHOSE The other form, *whose*, is tight and possessive,
namely, *whose life is it anyway? The man whose
car is parked over my driveway.*

It also extends to *your* and *you're*.

YOU'RE *you're* – means you are
        the apostrophe has taken the place of 'a'.
        For example: *You are a fine artist: you're a fine
                     artist.*
                     *You are a responsive audience:
                     you're a responsive audience.*

YOUR   The other form, *your*, is tight and possessive,
namely, *this is your book. I hope that you can
find your way home.*

A variation
It also extends to *there's* and *theirs*. Look at the apostrophe: we know this means a letter left out, therefore:

THERE'S   *there's – means there is*
          The apostrophe has taken the place of the 'i'.
          For example: *There is no problem: there's no*
          problem.
          There is my missing wallet: there's
          my missing wallet.

THEIRS   The other form is tight and possessive, namely,
          this problem is theirs to solve.

They're, their and *there* are also confused sometimes.

THEY'RE   *There is an apostrophe, so it means that some-*
          thing has been missed out. In this case it is an
          'a'. They're means they are.
          For example: *They are going on holiday: they're*
          going on holiday.

THEIR   is tight and possessive.
          For example: *their house, their car, their*
          opinions.

THERE   is a place. The trick is to remember that the
          spelling is similar to *here*. When in doubt,
          remember *here and there*!

Split infinitives
Most of us have heard about them and we probably
know that they are a mistake, but what are they? Simply
speaking, the infinitive is the name we give to verbs –
action words – in their simple uninflected form, for
example: *to sing, to write, to walk*. Splitting an infinitive

means putting an adverb (or adverbial phrase) between the auxiliary verb (*to*) and the verb (*sing*), for example:

the right thing to now do – is a split infinitive, because the infinitive *to do* has been split up by the adverb *now*

the right thing to do now – avoids the split infinitive

you need to swiftly cut the cord – is also a split infinitive, because the infinitive *to cut* has been split by the adverb *swiftly*

you need to cut the cord swiftly – avoids the split infinitive

Technically, split infinitives are not really a mistake. Infinitives have been split since the 12th century, and have fallen in and out of common usage throughout the years. The argument against them is that the *to* plus the verb form a single unit, but this doesn't accord with other patterns in English where we're perfectly happy to separate verbs from their auxiliaries (for example, *I have always wanted . . .*). Even though there's no formal reason not to happily split infinitives, there is a social one, as many people find them ugly and, in some extreme cases, offensive. As a result, it's probably best to avoid them if you can.

Problem nouns and verbs
There is a small collection of nouns and verbs which frequently cause confusion because while they sound similar or the same, they have different meanings and different spellings. They are: *advice/advise*; *licence/license*; *practice/practise*. In each pairing, the first is the

noun, the naming word; the second is the verb, the action word.

Therefore:

ADVICE is the noun.	For example: *Let me give you some advice.*
ADVISE is the verb.	For example: *Let me advise you.*
LICENCE is the noun.	For example: *I am going to buy a TV licence.*
LICENSE is the verb.	For example: *I license you to shoot on in the woods.*
PRACTICE is the noun.	For example: *It's time for Sam's piano practice.*
PRACTISE is the verb.	For example: *Dr Smith practises general medicine.*

Advice/advise form the most useful pair to remember because the way we say the words is different. The Advice (pronounced *adv-ICE*) Centre is a place we go to. We hope that when we go there, someone will advise us (pronounced *adv-IZE*). If you can remember this, it will help set the pattern for the correct use of the other pairs of words, *licence/license* and *practice/practise*, which in each instance sound the same.

14.3 COMMONLY MISSPELT WORDS

acceptance	acknowledge
accommodate	acquaint
accommodation	acquaintance
accustomed	acquire

acquisition
admittance
advice (noun: for example,
   advice centre)
advise (verb: for example,
   I advise you)
ageing
agenda
aggravate
aggressive
analyse
analysis
anxious
appendices
authenticate
authoritative
believe
beneficial
benefited
benevolent
bizarre
bureaucracy
calculate
ceremonial
character
chauvinist
clauses
clichés
commercial
committee
comparative
computer

concept
confidential
connoisseur
consequence
controversy
coordination
deceit
deceptive
defective
deficient
definite
dependant (noun: meaning
   *someone who relies upon
   another*)
dependent (adjective: meaning
   unable to do without)
description
desperate
despicable
deteriorate
dialogue
dilemma
dimensions
disciplinary
dissatisfied
economical
embarrass
emotional
environment
erroneous
ethical
exaggerate

exceptional

exercise

extraordinary

facilitate

faithfully

feasible

fictional

fictitious

flagrant

flaunt

flout

fulfil

furore

government

gracious

grammar

graphic

harass

honorary

humorous

idiosyncrasy

illegal

illicit

immoral

immunity

impractical

inconceivable

incredible

ingenious

initiate

inquiry

interrogate

invaluable

irregular

judgement

judicial

legitimate

liaise

liaison

library

licence (noun: for example, *driving licence*)

license (verb: for example, *you license me to shoot grouse*)

literally

luxurious

malicious

millennium

miniature

mischievous

momentary

mortgage

naive

necessary

necessitate

noticeable

occasion

occurred

official

outrageous

parallel

perceptible

phenomenon

phonetics

possessive

practice (noun: for example, *doctor's practice*)

practise (verb: for example, *I practise the piano*)

precede

predicament

prefer

preferable

preparation

prestigious

principal (adjective: meaning *main*) (noun: meaning *head of educational establishment; leading actor*)

principle (noun: meaning *fundamental truth or standard*)

proceed

profession

prohibit

pronunciation

protagonist

questionnaire

queuing

receipt

reciprocal

recommend

refer

referred

regrettable

reimburse

relevant

relinquish

remittance

repercussion

repetitious

respectfully

respectively

restaurant

seize

separate

significant

sincerely

singular

skilful

sociable

stipulate

subordinate

substitute

supplement

supplementary

suspicious

technique

temporarily

temporary

truly

unique

viable

voluntary

whatever

whenever

whoever

withhold

Chapter summary

- For important letters, write a draft first, set it aside and read it again later
- Ask someone you trust to check the final version for spelling and grammar
- Don't rely on a computer spell-check. When in doubt, consult a good dictionary or thesaurus
- Keep it simple; short clear sentences are easier to read than long complicated ones
- Avoid abbreviations your recipient may not recognize, and ensure that your letter is well presented
- If you split an infinitive or misplace a semicolon, remember that people will still talk to you

Further Information

Agony Aunts
Parentline Plus
Free Helpline: 0808 800 2222
www.parentlineplus.org.uk
Relate
Phone during office hours: 01788 573241
Samaritans
24 hour telephone service: 708457 909090
Or write in confidence to jo@samaritans.org

Bereavement
British Association for Counselling & Psychotherapy
BACP House, 35–37 Albert Street, Rugby, Warwick-
shire CV21 2SG
Telephone: 0870 443 5252
www.bacp.co.uk
Cruse Bereavement Care
Telephone Helpline: 0870 167 1677
Young Person's Helpline (Free Phone) 0808 808 1677
www.helpline@crusebereavementcare.org.uk

Charities
www.allaboutgiving.org
www.justgiving.com

Complaints
Consumer Direct
08454 040506
Trading Standards
www.tradingstandards.gov.uk

Dictionaries and Reference Books
Encarta World English Dictionary, Kathy Rooney, Bloomsbury, 1999
The Penguin English Dictionary, Robert Allen, Penguin, 2004
The Penguin Pocket English Dictionary, Robert Allen, Penguin, 2004

The New Fowler's Modern English Usage, R. W. Burchfield, Oxford, 1998
The Penguin Thesaurus, Rosalind Fergusson, Martin Manser and David Pickering, Penguin, 2004
Roget's Thesaurus of English Words and Phrases, George Davidson, Penguin, 2003
Usage and Abusage, Eric Partridge, Penguin, 1999

How to Write and Speak Better, John Ellison-Kahn, Reader's Digest, 1991

Job Applications/References
CIPD: Chartered Institute of Personnel and Development
www.cipd.co.uk
Croner-i
www.croner-i.co.uk
The Penguin Guide to Employment Rights, Hina Belitz and Dominic Crossley-Holland, Penguin, 2006

Layout and Invitations
The Smythson Guide to Everyday Stationery, available from Smythson, 40 New Bond Street, W1S 2DE

Money
www.moneyclaim.gov.uk
www.payontime.co.uk
for checking credit/information on businesses:
www.dnbibl.com
Dun & Bradstreet International, Holmers Farm Way, High Wycombe, Buckinghamshire HP12 4UL
www.dnbibl.com
Experian, Talbot House, Talbot Street, Nottingham NG1 5HF
www.experian.co.uk

Networking and Good Manners:
Networking: The Art of Making Friends, Carole Stone, Vermilion, 2000
The Ultimate Guide to Successful Networking, Carole Stone, Vermilion, 2004

Titles and Forms of Address
Burke's Peerage, Baronetage and Knightage, Charles Mosley, The Boydell Press, updated regularly
Debrett's Correct Form, Headline, 2002
Titles and Forms of Address, A&C Black, 2002

Index